Order this book online at www.trafford.com/05-1977
or email orders@trafford.com

Most Trafford titles are also available at major online book retailers.

Note for Librarians: A cataloguing record for this book is available from Library
and Archives Canada at www.collectionscanada.ca/amicus/index-e.html

Printed in Victoria, BC, Canada.

ISBN: 978-1-4120-7066-9

*We at Trafford believe that it is the responsibility of us all, as both individuals
and corporations, to make choices that are environmentally and socially sound.
You, in turn, are supporting this responsible conduct each time you purchase a
Trafford book, or make use of our publishing services. To find out how you are
helping, please visit www.trafford.com/responsiblepublishing.html*

*Our mission is to efficiently provide the world's finest, most comprehensive
book publishing service, enabling every author to experience success.
To find out how to publish your book, your way, and have it available
worldwide, visit us online at www.trafford.com/10510*

www.trafford.com

North America & international
toll-free: 1 888 232 4444 (USA & Canada)
phone: 250 383 6864 ♦ fax: 250 383 6804
email: info@trafford.com

The United Kingdom & Europe
phone: +44 (0)1865 722 113 ♦ local rate: 0845 230 9601
facsimile: +44 (0)1865 722 868 ♦ email: info.uk@trafford.com

10 9 8 7 6 5 4 3 2 1

CHINA HOUSE

An Inside Look at the "New" People's Republic
of China and the Impending Downfall of the
Current Communist Dynasty

LAWRENCE KLEPINGER

Acknowledgements

I want to thank Jeff van Löben Sels for his time and consideration in designing and typesetting this book. Without his expertise this project would not have been possible. Also, I want to thank my wife, Akiko, for putting up with "endless" stacks of paper all over the floor of our cramped, Chinese dormitory for much longer than I had initially promised. Also to our daughter Mai, and our two grandsons, Yuuto and Emon, for all their help and understanding regarding getting this manuscript to print. And finally, to the great staff at Trafford Publishing for all their professional help and consideration.

Personal Dedication

CHINA HOUSE is expressly dedicated to all freedom loving Chinese people who desire a truly democratic society—which they so richly deserve.

But it is especially dedicated to my past Chinese university students. You taught me more than you can ever imagine. I promised that I would do my best to get the truth out about what is really going on inside China. I hope CHINA HOUSE helps, in some small way, to fulfill that obligation.

Thank you again for all your kind consideration and understanding.

I will never forget you—for *you*—not the government—are the future of China.

Keep thinking positive. And never give up!

TABLE OF CONTENTS

CHAPTER 2

CHAPTER 3

CHAPTER 4

The Beginning of the Systematic Governmental
Abandonment of the People by the Chinese
Communist Party

CHAPTER 5

CHAPTER 6

CHAPTER 7

CHAPTER 8

CHAPTER 9

CHAPTER 10

Please Read This First

I have no illusions about the "fact" that I will be taken to task for writing this book. I have already been warned by countless Chinese friends, along with my teaching colleagues, that it is not a very good idea to put all this down on paper.

"Besides," chided one of the more cynical, seasoned veteran teachers, "nobody's going to believe you anyway—much less, give a damn."

That is probably true. However, I feel an obligation to write what I witnessed in China in hopes of helping others that come after me, and there will be a boatload of people that follow, just as I have, in dealing with what they are about to experience.

I have written the truth as I saw it. I ask all people who are planning on coming to China to check with others who have been there for an extended period of time—not the ones who have been on the *Foreigner's Tour* and think they know it all—to check my ideas and concepts and see if what I am saying is true or off the mark.

Suffice it to say, China is on the move. But that does not mean it is without enormous problems that are being intentionally ignored by the mainstream media—for fear of losing "favor" in the eyes of the Chinese Communist Party (CCP), and thus perhaps being shut out of one of the truly great stories of the 21st Century—the emergence of the "New" China.

But just like in the 1980s, with all the nonsense of Japan as number one, the intellectual elite, along with their government-financed counterparts, lack the courage to really lay out what is wrong with China, choosing instead to climb onto the bandwagon and tout the "great strides" that China is making, while ignoring critical signs of danger on the not too distant horizon.

More often than not, this attitude of selective objectivity is due to the enormously large amounts of money that people can make by saying only "good things" about China.

If you are generous with praise then you are escorted around like royalty, treated to the best restaurants and offered lucrative speaking engagements at all the choice universities and posh business clubs in China, as was Ezra Vogel when he was ushered around Japan peddling his book, *Japan as Number One*, while at the same time competing for the affections of the Japanese "elite" and the money they gave him to perpetuate his ill-conceived notion of Japan becoming the next world economic superpower.

That was just before Japan's economic bubble burst and the Japanese stock market, along with the real estate market, lost almost 70% of its value, crashing into an economic downturn that has lasted for over a decade. It is just now beginning to emerge from that financial abyss.

But Mr. Vogel doesn't care. He got rich off the scam—and saw the world on someone else's dime while doing so. I am afraid it is happening again, in China.

Not one of the mainstream media is telling the whole truth about what is really going on. Just bits and pieces when they come to light. Thus, my attempting to fill in the gaps with this book.

In the People's Republic of China, it is very hard to get facts and figures when what is printed in both academic journals and the government controlled press treat the truth as an unwelcome stepchild.

I have no axe to grind with China—nor the Chinese people. All I am doing is presenting the things I saw, simply as I saw them.

Do I have facts and figures to back up *everything* I have written about? Absolutely not.

When you live in a country that openly extinguishes freedom of press, freedom of expression and freedom of individual thought—what good are government authorized "facts?"

Not even the Chinese people are foolish enough to believe what they read in their own newspapers. So why should I?

And if anybody should know, it is the Chinese people themselves. After all, it is their country—not mine.

CHINA HOUSE is not meant to be an academic treatise about China. Far from it. We have enough of those already—with varying degrees of inaccuracy.

Rather, this book is solely intended for the "average person" to get a quick idea of what the "New" China is really all about.

I am not going to waste the reader's time with unnecessary digressions about the "Emerging Chinese Giant" nor any other media generated hype that so many unsuspecting visitors to the Middle Kingdom accept as Gospel.

This book will attempt to dispel the plethora of *myth-information* that has been perpetuated by the fawning news organizations of the world in hopes of currying favor with the present Chinese communist status quo—for purely monetary considerations.

You will find in this book information that other publications— and writers—simply don't have the courage to put into print, for fear of public scorn, physical retaliation, or the worst punishment of all—denial to take part in the great economic expansion that is now happening in China.

Sometimes just straightforward, gut-level, empirical evidence will convey a situation much better than convoluted academic jargon or guarded diplomatic platitudes.

My purpose is to inform—not to insult—nor ridicule. I do not take a Politically Correct approach in this book, so be prepared for the truth—as it presented itself to me—and countless other "foreign experts" that have lived and worked in China.

When dealing with any culture it becomes necessary to use generalizations—especially with a country that has 5,000 years of history, the third/fourth largest landmass in the world, and the biggest population to boot. For this I am sorry.

Also, my heartfelt apologies to any referenced material that may not be correctly cited. I have tried to give credit to the appropriate sources, but I realize I have not done so in the strictest of academic protocol. I personally feel that referenced, properly cited sources make one's manuscript more valid and much easier to defend.

On occasion, when researching data on the Internet, as soon as I finished reading certain articles and then went back to cite the source, the article had already been removed by the Chinese Internet Propaganda Police.

For the sake of readability, I have purposely not used either the APA or Chicago style of referencing.

To all authors that I have failed to give proper credit, I am sincerely sorry. Please help me to see my oversights and I will gladly correct them in future presentations.

If there are any comments or suggestions, please e-mail me at:

lawrenceklepinger@gmail.com

Finally, if this book makes for better communication and a clearer understanding of what is really going on in the "New" China then I will consider my efforts well spent.

Welcome to CHINA HOUSE.

Before We Begin—The Constant Chinese "Variable"—*Face*

To know any country, and how it functions, you first have to be aware of some basic ground rules.

In China, *Face*, is paramount above all else. Above business matters. Above family obligations. Above personal relationships. Self-pride rules.

Face permeates every nook and cranny, every discussion, every business conference, public or private. It is predominant at all levels.

One could actually make a case by stating that, from the poorest of the poor to the richest of the rich, *Face* is the ONLY factor governing Chinese life.

If a Chinese person's *Face* is ever threatened, or actually disgraced, they will remember it forever, waiting for a chance to "regain" their perceived lost pride. There is no exception to this rule.

The concept of *Face* will be revisited throughout this book, either by subtle implication or outright comment, it is that intrinsic in the cultural psyche of the Chinese people.

With this basic concept in mind, let us proceed.

CHAPTER 1

SOME CURRENT BASIC INFORMATION

Anniversary of the founding of the People's Republic of China (PRC): October 1, 1949

Chief of State: President Hu Jintao, since 15 March 2003

Head of Government: Premier Wen Jiabao, since 16 March 2003

Chinese Communist Party (CCP) and the National People's Congress (NPC) are the official designations.

The Politburo consists of a seven-member Standing Committee that is elected by the CCP Central Committee.

Population

1,313,973,713 (July 2006 est.)

China contains more than one-fifth of the world's entire human population.

More than one-fourth of its population is under 15 years of age.

Geographic Size

3,705,392 square miles

Aksai Chin and Trans-Karakoram Tracts are both territories claimed by India.

Other disputed territories include Taiwan, Penghu, Kinmen and Matsu which the Republic of China (Taiwan) has continued to govern after the People's Republic of China (PRC) replaced it on the mainland.

Beijing (capital) 11,250,000

Shanghai 13,560,000

Countries Bordering China

North Korea, Taiwan (100 miles off the coast of Fujian Province), Vietnam, Laos, Myanmar, India, Bhutan, Nepal, Afghanistan, Tajikistan, Kyrgyzstan, Kazakhstan, Russia, Mongolia, and Pakistan

Some Chief Crops:

Rice, potatoes, tobacco, cotton, sorghum, peanuts

Some Major Industries:

Iron, steel, coal

Labor Force:

800 million

Imports:

Japan, Germany, Taiwan, South Korea and the USA

Exports:

Hong Kong, Japan, Germany, South Korea, and the USA

Suffrage

18 years of age; universal

Outlying Regions

Hong Kong and Macau are considered Special Administrative Regions of the People's Republic of China, with their own respective flags.

Tibet is considered a province-level autonomous region of the People's Republic of China but still in dispute with the Dalai Lama, along with many Tibetan people both within the country and in exile.

Taiwan considers itself an independent nation—but Mainland China disputes this claim and has threatened military intervention if Taiwan moves to declare total independence. Eventually, the PRC desires to make Taiwan a part of its "one country, two systems" policy that Hong Kong and Macao are now compelled to operate under.

NOTE: Do not confuse the People's Republic of China (PRC) with the Republic of China (ROC), which is Taiwan.

SOURCES:

Wikipedia, The Free Encyclopedia, from the Internet at:
http://en.wikipedia.org/wiki/List_of_countries_by_area

The World Factbook, from the Internet at:
http://www.cia.gov/cia/publications/factbook/geos/ch.html

The New Encyclopedia Britannica, Volume 3, 15th Edition, 2005, pp 221–230

The New York Times Almanac, 2007

PRELUDE TO A FEW HISTORICAL FACTS

To put CHINA HOUSE into perspective, with relation to the Chinese concept of how they perceive the world and their everyday social condition, the following historical events are referred to:

A Brief Review of Chinese Dynasties

A Brief Chronology of Chinese Natural Disasters

A Brief Chronology of "Recent" Catastrophic Chinese Political Events

Comments Regarding Certain Sections of the Constitution of the People's Republic of China

A Closer Look at the Chinese Communist Flag—Article 136

NOTE: The main focus of this brief outline is primarily to draw attention to the ever-pressing problem of *Dynastic Change* in conjunction with the unrelenting population of the people, coupled with its relationship to the "survival of the fittest" mentality that has been continually present in China down through the centuries, from the first dynastic order to the present-day Communist Dynasty.

Once the reader gets an idea of the enormity of death, mayhem, chaos and destruction that has permeated Chinese history from the outset, with numbing regularity, it is hoped that a different perspective will come to light with regard to what is actually happening in today's "New" China.

A BRIEF REVIEW OF CHINESE DYNASTIES

THE EARLY DYNASTIES:

2000–1500 B.C.	Xia Dynasty
1550–1055 B.C.	Shang Dynasty
1055–771 B.C.	Western Zhou Dynasty
770–221 B.C.	Eastern Zhou Dynasty
770–476 B.C.	Spring and Autumn Period
481–256 B.C.	Warring States Period
221–207 B.C.	Qin Dynasty
206 B.C.–A.D. 9	Western Han Dynasty
A.D. 25–220	Eastern Han Dynasty
A.D. 220–265	**THREE KINGDOMS DYNASTIES:**
220–265	Wei Dynasty
221–263	Shu Dynasty
229–280	Wu Dynasty
A.D. 265–316	Western Jin Dynasty
A.D. 317–420	Eastern Jin Dynasty
A.D. 424–535	Northern Wei Dynasty

A.D. 420–588	SOUTHERN DYNASTIES:
420–478	Song Dynasty
479–501	Qi Dynasty
502–556	Liang Dynasty
557–588	Chen Dynasty
A.D. 386–588	NORTHERN DYNASTIES:
386–533	Northern Wei Dynasty
534–549	Eastern Wei Dynasty
535–557	Western Wei Dynasty
550–577	Northern Qi Dynasty
557–588	Northern Zhou Dynasty
A.D. 589–617	Sui Dynasty
A.D. 618–907	Tang Dynasty
A.D. 907–960	FIVE DYNASTIES:
907–923	Later Liang Dynasty
923–936	Later Tang Dynasty
936–946	Later Jin Dynasty
947–950	Later Han Dynasty
951–960	Later Zhou Dynasty

A.D. 907–979	Ten Kingdoms Dynasties
A.D. 960–1279	**SONG DYNASTY:**
960–1127	Northern Song Dynasty
1127–1279	Southern Song Dynasty
A.D. 916–1125	**LIAO DYNASTY**
A.D. 1038–1227	**WESTERN XIA DYNASTY**
A.D. 1115–1234	**JIN DYNASTY**
A.D. 1279–1368	**YUAN DYNASTY** (Mongol Dynasty)
A.D. 1368–1644	**MING DYNASTY**
A.D. 1644–1911	**QING DYNASTY** (Manchu Dynasty)
A.D. 1911–1949	**REPUBLIC OF CHINA** (Mainland China)
A.D. 1949	**PEOPLE'S REPUBLIC OF CHINA** (Mainland, Hong Kong, Macao)
A.D. 1949	**REPUBLIC OF CHINA** (Taiwan)

NOTE: There is considerable disagreement among historians as to when the earlier dynasties actually appeared, so this order may differ from other chronological listings, as well as some of the English spellings. However, it serves the purpose in showing the magnitude of historical change that has plagued China since its very inception.

SOURCES:

http://www.chaos.umd.edu/history/time_line.html

New York Times 2006, 2007 Almanacs

A BRIEF CHRONOLOGY OF CHINESE NATURAL DISASTERS

A.D. 1290   Chihli Earthquake: 100,000 deaths

A.D. 1556   Shaanxi Earthquake (considered the world's worst
                     earthquake measured in deaths): 825,000 deaths

A.D. 1642   Kaifeng Flood: 295,000 deaths

A.D 1731   Beijing Earthquake: 100,000 deaths

A.D. 1876–1879   Northern China Drought: 12 million deaths

A.D. 1887   Huang He/Yellow River Flood: 1.5 million deaths

A.D. 1892–1896   Bubonic Plague: 10 million deaths

A.D. 1907   Famine: 20 million deaths

A.D. 1911   Chang Jiang/Yangtze River Flood: 100,000 deaths

A.D. 1920   Gansu Earthquake: 200,000 deaths

A.D. 1927   Nanshan Earthquake: 200,000 deaths

A.D. 1928–1930   Honan and Kansu Drought: 3 million deaths

A.D. 1931   Huang He/Yellow River Flood: 3.5 million deaths

A.D. 1932   Gansu Earthquake: 70,000 deaths

A.D. 1935   Chang Jiang/Yangtze River Flood: 140,000 deaths

A.D. 1936   Western China Drought: 5 million deaths

A.D. 1938   Huang He/Yellow River Flood: 850,000 deaths

A.D. 1941	Drought: 3 million deaths
A.D. 1954	Chang Jiang/Yangtze River Flood: 30,000 deaths
A.D. 1958–1962	Famine (considered the world's worst famine, in which starvation, disease, chaos, and cannibalism ensued): 20 million deaths*
A.D. 1975	Typhoon Nina: 230,000 deaths
A.D. 1976	Tangshan Earthquake: 700,000 deaths

NOTE: The actual death tolls of these disasters are often in dispute by the ruling communist party for obvious reasons. But any way you look at it, what is not in dispute is the horrendous number of people that were killed as a result of these natural calamities.

*During this time period China was virtually closed off to the West. These figures were not released to the "outside" world until mid-year 1981.

SOURCE:

New York Times 2006 Almanac

A BRIEF CHRONOLOGY OF "RECENT" CATASTROPHIC POLITICAL EVENTS

A.D. 1819 East India Company—which was owned and operated by the British, began to import opium into China under the aegis of trying to balance the tea trade, but in actuality it was undertaken in hopes of controlling certain aspects of Chinese society. The importation of opium became such a scourge that it almost ruined the entire country.

A.D. 1839–1842 1st Opium War—in which China lost and was forced to accept the Treaty of Nanjing, signed in 1842, ceding Hong Kong to the British. The Chinese were also forced to sign the British Supplementary Treaty of the Bogue in 1843. The British accomplished this, in part, by bribing the ruling Chinese clan to betray their own country—and the people. Also, the Chinese were not adept at "modern" military warfare and lost almost every battle they fought with the superior foreign invaders.

A.D. 1856–1860 2nd Opium War—China defeated by military forces and coerced into accepting, yet again, another treaty, this time the Treaty of Tianjin imposed on them by Britain, with the allied help of Russia, the USA and France, allowing foreign dignitaries into the country, legalizing Christianity—yet still making the importation of opium legal in China. When China tried to resist, the British and French destroyed the Summer Palace and the Chinese were forced to abide by the terms of the Treaty of Tianjin and make even more concessions to the occupying forces. In effect, the Chinese, to this day, consider these two wars as the most humiliating defeats in their entire history. In private, many historians maintain that this feeling derives from the fact that both defeats were at the hands of "white" Westerners and therefore only adds to the immense loss of international *Face* the Chinese feel they have unjustly suffered.

A.D. 1894–1895 Sino-Japanese War—China defeated by Japan and forced to cede Seoul, Korea and Formosa (Taiwan) to the Japanese. After this defeat other nations moved into China to divide the country into colonies of their own, Britain, Germany and Russia being the main culprits to take advantage of China's decline.

A.D. 1900 The Boxer Rebellion—was put down by alien forces and, as a result, China was further carved up by invading states, virtually rendering it completely divided into foreign occupational forces.

A.D. 1911–1912 Republic of China—was temporarily established by Sun Yat-sen, thus ending the last Emperor ruling class in China. In the eyes of many, Sun Yat-sen was the real "father of modern China," not Mao Zedong.

A.D. 1916–1926 Wars of the Warlords—took place, thus ending China's brief encounter with a democratic-republican form of government.

A.D. 1926 Chinese Civil War—again broke out among differing factions, Nationalists and Communists, left and right wing groups, trying to control China and the fate of its future.

A.D. 1931 Japanese Invasion of Manchuria—Japan invaded on September 18 and established the puppet state of Manchuguo (Manchuria) and began full-scale occupation of the eastern coastal regions of China.

A.D. 1931–1945 Slave Labor—Chinese women forced into prostitution to sexually service Japanese soldiers during World War II. Chinese men made to work as slave laborers for Japanese companies or shipped to Hokkaido, Japan, to work in coal mines. Hundreds of thousands of men and women died of mistreatment and starvation during this period of history. Japan still refuses to acknowledge, apologize or compensate for their part in these wartime atrocities.

A.D. 1935–1945 Japanese Biological Warfare Unit 731—disguised as a water-purification center, the infamous testing unit was established in China where vivisections were performed on a daily basis and biological experiments were conducted on live Chinese peasants, as well as other nationalities, that had been taken prisoners of war by the occupying Japanese forces. Various diseases were developed, including bubonic plague and anthrax and released on Chinese soldiers, civilians and POWs alike. It is virtually unknown how many innocent people were killed in the process.[1]

A.D. 1937 Nanjing Massacre—took place in which approximately 300,000 Chinese were massacred by Japanese forces. Mass live burials to save ammunition, wanton murder, rape and pillage rampaged on for weeks unabated. To this day, the Japanese government insists that the "incident" never happened.

A.D. 1946–1949 Chinese Civil War—Mao Zedong and the communist Chinese win control of the mainland and establish the People's Republic of China; Chiang Kai-shek forced to abandon the mainland and retreat to Formosa (Taiwan) to establish the Republic of China. The communists refer to this period as the "War of Liberation."

A.D. 1958–1962 Great Leap Forward—"Failed industrialization campaign undertaken by the Chinese communists between 1958 and early 1960. Mao Zedong hoped to develop labor-intensive methods of industrialization that would emphasize manpower rather than the gradual purchase of heavy machinery, thereby putting to use China's dense population and obviating the need to accumulate capital. Rather than large new factories, he proposed developing backyard steel furnaces in every village. Rural people were organized into communes where agricultural and political decisions emphasized ideological purity rather than expertise. The program was implemented so hastily and zealously that many errors occurred; these were exacerbated by a series of natural disasters and the withdrawal of Soviet technical personnel. China's agriculture was so disrupted that about 20 million people died of starvation from 1958 to 1962. By early 1960 the government began to repeal the Great Leap Forward; private plots were returned to peasants and expertise began to be emphasized again."[2]

A.D. 1966–1976 Cultural Revolution—"Upheaval launched by Mao Zedong to renew the spirit of revolution in China. Mao feared urban social stratification in a society as traditionally elitist as China and also believed that programs instituted to correct for the failed Great Leap Forward showed that his colleagues lacked commitment to the revolution. He organized China's urban youths into groups called the Red Guards, shut down China's schools, and encouraged the Red Guards to attack all traditional values and 'bourgeois things.' They soon splintered into zealous rival groups, and in 1968 Mao sent millions of them to the rural hinterland, bringing some order to the cities. Within the government, a coalition of Mao's associates fought with more moderate elements, many of whom were purged, were verbally attacked, were physically abused, and subsequently died; leaders Liu Shaoqi and Lin Biao both died under mysterious circumstances. From 1973 to Mao's death in 1976, politics shifted between the hard-line Gang of Four and the moderates headed by Zhou Enlai and Deng Xiaoping. After Mao's death the Cultural Revolution was brought to a close. By that time, nearly three million party members and countless wrongfully purged citizens awaited reinstatement. The Cultural Revolution subsequently was repudiated in China."[3]

A.D. 1989 Tiananmen Square Massacre—on June 3–4 violent clashes with police and military left hundreds of pro-democracy students dead in the streets—a historical fact that has been very discretely removed from all Chinese school textbooks. In other words, it didn't happen—much like the Japanese government's official proclamation that the Nanjing Massacre never took place.

SOURCES:

[1] JAPANESE BIOLOGICAL WARFARE UNIT 731:

Harris, Sheldon H., *Factories of Death*, Rutledge, 1994

Daws, Gavin, *Prisoners of the Japanese: POWS of World War II in the Pacific*, William Morrow, 1994

[2] GREAT LEAP FORWARD, [3] CULTURAL REVOLUTION:

Encyclopedia Britannica, both direct quotes verbatim, Internet. http://www.answers.com/topic/great-leap-forward

COMMENTS REGARDING CERTAIN SECTIONS OF THE CONSTITUTION OF THE PEOPLE'S REPUBLIC OF CHINA

Each time there was a dynastic change in China the rules were re-written, property confiscated, people put to death, status quo realignments and the like. The concept of law, based on a single, written constitution that has been handed down through the ages, is simply not a part of the Chinese cultural heritage.

Although the present Chinese Communist Party (CCP) does have a written constitution it is so biased in favor of the ruling status quo, and patently disregarded by the government whenever the need arises, that it is of very little value to the people themselves.

The so-called "good points" that once existed for the people's benefit, under socialism, have been permanently expunged from the "New" China of today—yet the slave/state mentality still remains. This will become painfully clear in the sections that follow.

In actuality, this is not a constitution of the "people." It is a

Proclamation of the Chinese Communist Party to obey—or else.

NOTE: Words and phrases in "**bold**" type are directly taken from the Chinese constitution. All instances of italicized, bold type of the word *state* are that of the author.

The Preamble

In the Preamble to the Constitution of the People's Republic of China, which was adopted on December 4, 1982, reference is made to how the Chinese have a "**glorious revolutionary tradition.**"

Revolutionary, yes. Glorious—not by a long shot.

In every revolution the people of China paid the ultimate price only to see themselves, time and again, come under yet another dynasty of cruelty, crime, corruption and one agonizingly bribe-ridden bureaucracy after another. The current Communist Dynasty is no different.

The Preamble goes on, in the most classic of oxymoronic statements ever inserted into a national constitution, when it brazenly purports that, "**The people's democratic dictatorship led by the working class and based on the alliance of workers and peasants, which is, in essence, the dictatorship of the proletariat, has been consolidated and developed.**"

It would be extremely interesting to hear a debate on what a "democratic dictatorship" really is—let alone how it is chosen, not to mention by which it operates.

The Preamble further states that—and this point is missed by many who are so enamored with the "democratization" that is supposedly taking place in China today—"**after the founding of the People's Republic, the transition of Chinese society from a new democratic, to a socialist society, was effected step by step.**"

It is not that the CCP wants to go *from* communism to a democracy. Quite the opposite is true.

The Chinese Communist Party intends to lead the people *away* from democracy and back into totalitarian enslavement. This is their stated goal, effectively codified in their national constitution.

The Preamble goes on to say that, **"an independent and fairly comprehensive socialist system of industry has, in the main, been established. There has been a marked increase in agricultural production. Significant progress has been made in educational, scientific, cultural and other undertakings, and socialist ideological education has yielded noteworthy results."**

The most "noteworthy result" of its "socialist ideological education" system is that it has indoctrinated its charges with a skewed version of world-accepted historical facts.

That does not equate to a "noteworthy result." What it does prove is how rigid and conformist the educational/indoctrinational process that currently exists in China actually is.

Furthermore, the Preamble points out that, **"the Chinese people took state power into their own hands and became masters of the country"** and further proclaims that, **"major successes have been achieved in economic development and the living standards of the people have improved considerably."**

The Chinese people did not take state power into their own hands.

The Chinese Communist Party confiscated it—and by sheer bully exploitation still retains that power.

And the living standards of the people haven't improved that much, not when you consider that out of a population of 1.3 *billion* there are 1,000,000,000 people still living at or below the subsistence level.

Ask the average Chinese person on the street if they have the power of government in their own hands and they will laugh at you.

But probably the most disturbing part of the Preamble is the innocuous sentence that proclaims, "**The exploiting classes, as such, have been eliminated in our country.**"

Nothing could be further from the truth, yet it is right there in the preamble to the constitution.

In truth, the largest exploiting class that exists today is that of the Chinese Communist Party.

Further into the Preamble, Taiwan is specifically referred to, thus attesting to its perceived importance to Mainland China, and the *Face* that surrounds the whole issue when it is stated that, "**Taiwan is part of the sacred territory of the People's Republic of China. It is the lofty duty of the entire Chinese people, including our compatriots in Taiwan, to accomplish the great task of reunifying the motherland. In building socialism, it is imperative to rely on the workers, peasants and intellectuals and unite with all the forces that can be united. In the long years of revolution and construction, there has been formed under the leadership of the Communist Party of China a broad, patriotic, united front that is composed of democratic parties and people's organizations and embraces all socialist working people, all patriots who support socialism and all patriots who stand for reunification of the motherland. This united front will continue to be consolidated and developed.**"

When you consider the impact of the above quote it is actually very shocking, but not with respect that China wants to be unified with Taiwan. That is pretty much a given, at least to mainlanders.

The shock comes from the blurring of the CCP (the state), with that of the people. It is a very clever way of melding the two into one, when the situation dictates it is best for the communist government's advantage, but strictly separating them anytime it suits their needs, most notably in the sharing of power in the basic sense of any truly democratic society.

CHAPTER I. GENERAL PRINCIPLES OF THE CONSTITUTION OF THE PEOPLE'S REPUBLIC OF CHINA

Article 1.

The last line of this article says, "**Sabotage of the socialist system by any organization or individual is prohibited.**"

Notice the word "individual." And this is only the first article. In essence, individual protest is against the law in China.

Article 4.

"**All nationalities in the People's Republic of China are equal.... The people of all nationalities have the freedom to use and develop their own spoken and written languages, and to preserve or reform their own ways and customs.**"

This simply is not true. The right of eminent domain rides rough-shod in China. If people, and their ethnic groups, refuse to move for one reason or another, they are summarily evicted, displaced—and forgotten. The Three Gorges Dam is a perfect example of this type of disregard for other people's "ways and customs."

It is estimated that hundreds of temples, thousands of burial sites, along with approximately a dozen cities, over 100 towns, and more than 1200 villages have been destroyed in the wake of the dam's construction.

Article 9.

"**Mineral resources, waters, forests, mountains, grassland, beaches and other natural resources are owned by the *state*...**"

Article 10.

"**Land in the cities is owned by the *state*...no organization or** individual may appropriate, buy, sell or lease land, or unlawfully transfer land in other ways. All organizations and individuals who use land must make rational use of the land."

The phrase "rational use" is not defined, thus subject to case-by-case interpretation. When I pointed this out to a Chinese colleague he shrugged his shoulders and grinned, then commented, "That way the state employee can make it appear that he is doing the person a favor by granting special permission to do something—thus making a good case for an under-the-table payoff."

Article 12.

"Appropriation or damage of *state* or collective property by any organization or individual by whatever means is prohibited."

Article 13.

"The *state* protects, by law, the right of citizens to inherit private property."

If this doesn't strike you as odd, it should. In effect, this article was a compromise to the ultra-rich elite of China, who still actually control much of the wealth in the country. Simply put, if the Chinese Communist Party didn't include this article into the constitution, thus granting the *Taipans* of China some assurance of their economic legacy being passed down through the ages, the ultra-rich that are still on the mainland would have left long ago.

Few people even know this article is part of the Chinese constitution—because only the ultra-rich in China have anything worth inheriting.

Article 14.

"The *state* continuously raises labor productivity..."

Article 15.

"The *state* practices economic planning on the basis of socialist public ownership..."

Article 16.

"*State* enterprises have decision-making power in operation and management within the limits prescribed by law..."

Article 19.

"The *state* develops socialist educational undertakings and works to raise the scientific and cultural level of the whole nation. The *state* runs schools of various types...the *state* develops educational facilities..."

Article 20.

"The *state* promotes the development of the natural and social sciences, disseminates scientific and technical knowledge..."

Article 21.

"The *state* develops medical and health services..."

Article 22.

"The *state* promotes the development of literature and art, the press, broadcasting and television undertakings, publishing and distribution services, libraries, museums, cultural centers and other cultural undertakings..."

Article 23.

"The *state* trains specialized personnel in all fields who serve socialism..."

Article 24.

"The *state* strengthens the building of socialist spiritual civilization..."

Article 25.

"The *state* promotes family planning so that population growth may fit the plans for economic and social development."

Article 26.

"The *state* protects and improves the living environment and the ecological environment, and prevents and controls pollution and other public hazards. The *state* organizes and encourages reforestation and the protection of forests."

This is probably one of the most blatant lies contained in the constitution. By any standard of measurement, China is one of the most environmentally polluted countries in the world.

Article 27.

"All *state* organs carry out the principle of simple and efficient administration..."

This *is* the biggest lie in the constitution. The bureaucratic nightmare that goes on unabated at all levels of government is legendary and completely true. Graft, crime and corruption are a fact of everyday life. If you know someone—or have enough money—the system works magnificently. If you don't have connections, you are out of luck.

Article 28.

"The *state* maintains public order and suppresses treasonable and other counter-revolutionary activities; it penalizes actions that endanger public security and disrupt the socialist economy and other criminal activities, and punishes and reforms criminals."

What is ingenious about this constitution is the vagueness in which the whole document is written. Time and again the careful reader comes across ambiguous words and phrases such as "treasonable and *other* counter-revolutionary activities." This type of writing is purposely all-encompassing and has no legal boundaries. In other words, it is left up to interpretation—again the implementation of law on a case-by-case basis—thus negating the effectiveness of a written constitution in even the broadest sense of the word.

Article 30.

"The administrative division of the People's Republic of China is as follows: (1) The country is divided into provinces, autonomous regions and municipalities directly under the Central Government; (2) Provinces and autonomous regions are divided into autonomous prefectures, counties, autonomous counties and cities; (3) Counties and autonomous counties are divided into townships, nationality townships and towns. Municipalities directly under the Central Government and other large cities are divided into districts and counties. Autonomous prefectures are divided into counties, autonomous counties, and cities. All autonomous regions, autonomous prefectures and autonomous counties are national autonomous areas."

I have included this in its entirety to show just how extensive the control of the country really is. What is not mentioned in the constitution is that you need special permission to travel to—and from—certain parts of China. You can't just jump into the car and go on a picnic anywhere you want.

It is also striking that some regions are divided into "nationality townships." This sounds akin to reservations or government designated special areas to me and doesn't jibe with the constitutional statement of treating everyone equally, regardless of their national origin.

CHAPTER II. THE FUNDAMENTAL RIGHTS AND DUTIES OF CITIZENS

Article 34.

"All citizens of the People's Republic of China who have reached the age of 18 have the right to vote...except persons deprived of political rights according to law."

Here again, this is a catch-all phrase that enables the government to lock up anybody they feel is working against the status quo.

Article 35.

"Citizens of the People's Republic of China enjoy freedom of speech, of the press, of assembly, of association, of procession and of demonstration."

Blatant lie. Tiananmen Square pro-democracy demonstrations and subsequent student massacre, 1989.

Article 36.

"Citizens of the People's Republic of China enjoy freedom of religious belief. No state organ, public organization or individual may compel citizens to believe in, or not to believe in, any religion; nor may they discriminate against citizens who believe in, or do not believe in, any religion..."

Blatant lie. The on-going officially sanctioned persecution of the Falun Gong, of Tibetan culture and continuous harassment of Chinese Catholics are but a few of the most extreme examples. The communist government actively prohibits Chinese Catholics from obeying the Holy See and instead invoke their own brand of forced *Chinese Catholocism* under the Catholic Patriotic Association of which a number of prominent Catholic bishops are currently under arrest for not adhering to the dictates of this official government body.

In an article entitled, "Praying for China," in the *Wall Street Journal*, Wednesday, June 20, 2007, it states that, "Christians of all denominations are still persecuted unless they worship in a party monitored church...Buddhists and adherents to other religions also cannot worship freely."

Government "observers" are always in attendance at Catholic, Christian, and other religious gatherings, so much so that practitioners are again retreating underground for fear of communist reprisals.

Article 37.

"The freedom of person of citizens of the People's Republic of China is inviolable...unlawful deprivation or restriction of citizens' freedom of person by detention or other means is prohibited; and unlawful search of the person of citizens is prohibited."

When I asked about this type of protection to my Chinese friends they looked askance, then chuckled to themselves. "The Chinese Military go anywhere they please," was the most common response.

Article 38.

"The personal dignity of citizens of the People's Republic of China is inviolable. Insult, libel, false charge or frame-up directed against citizens by any means is prohibited."

False charges and frame-ups directed at Chinese citizens is part of the communist political landscape, for without this form of constant intimidation the CCP, and its tyrannical grip on the people, would cease to exist.

Article 39.

"The home of citizens of the People's Republic of China is inviolable. Unlawful search of, or intrusion into, a citizen's home is prohibited."

Not true by any stretch of the imagination. Peoples' land and homes are confiscated on a regular basis—many times without fair compensation and sometimes without any prior notice. The tractors just show up and start bulldozing.

Article 40.

"The freedom and privacy of correspondence of citizens of the People's Republic of China are protected by law. No organization or individual may, on any grounds, infringe upon the freedom and privacy of citizens' correspondence except in cases where, to meet the needs of *state* security or of investigation into criminal offences, public security organizations are permitted to censor correspondence in accordance with procedures prescribed by law."

Letters coming in and going out of China are routinely checked on the grounds of "state security." Many postal employees take it upon themselves to pilfer money and other material goods from letters and packages, store them in the name of the state, then take them home as one of the many perks of working for the CCP.

Article 44.

"The *state* prescribes by law the system of retirement for workers and staff in enterprises and undertakings and for functionaries of organs of *state*. The livelihood of retired personnel is ensured by the *state* and society."

Here you have, in one short declaration, why everybody wants to work for the state. China is a nation of *pension pimps* par excellence and every Chinese person who is fortunate enough to be hired by the state jealously guards that position of privilege with frightening vengeance. Any job with the CCP is a license to steal from the people—and steal from the people they do.

Article 45.

"Citizens of the People's Republic of China have the right to material assistance from the *state* and society when they are old, ill or disabled.

The *state* develops the social insurance, social relief and medical and health services that are required to enable citizens to enjoy this right. The *state* and society ensure the livelihood of disabled members of the armed forces, provide pensions to the families of martyrs and give preferential treatment to the families of military personnel. The *state* and society help make arrangements for the work, livelihood and education of the blind, deaf, mute and other handicapped citizens."

This sounds very appealing. The only problem is, it's not true—and the Chinese people are extremely angry that this is no longer the case.

Most all medical relief and healthcare services are now administered through private insurance companies. If you don't have insurance you get no help.

While in China I saw more deaf, blind, and disabled people begging for money than I have anywhere else in the world. Legions of physically and mentally destitute people wander the streets of China with little or no hope of any relief whatsoever from the communist government, eking out a living scrounging table scraps from garbage cans, picking fruit from city trees and peddling it on the streets, with begging in all ways, shapes and forms rounding out the method of scraping out even the most meager of livelihoods.

Article 46.

"Citizens of the People's Republic of China have the duty as well as the right to receive education…"

Education is no longer free in China. Many girls, especially in the countryside, are denied the right to the most basic essentials of education on purely economic grounds.

Article 48.

"Women in the People's Republic of China enjoy equal rights with men in all spheres of life, political, economic, cultural and social, and family life…"

In an article by Christopher Allen entitled, *Traditions Weigh on China's Women*, he points out that, "In China, one woman kills herself every four minutes."

The article goes on to state that, "According to World Health Organization statistics, China is the only country in the world where more women commit suicide than men.

"Every year, 1.5 million women attempt to take their own lives, and a further 150,000 succeed in doing so."

I would venture a guess that the number is much higher, but that suicide is not listed as the real cause of death. Rather, many deaths are ruled to be of "natural causes."

Mr. Allen goes on by stating, "The problem is worse in rural areas, where the suicide rate is three times higher than in the cities.

"Suicide attempts may often be impulsive, but they are the result of burdens that weigh heavily on the shoulders of rural women." [1]

In a BBC television broadcast entitled, *China in the Country*, it pointed out that, "Marriage is a big issue where traditional attitudes still prevail.

"Many marriages are arranged and operate like business deals in which the groom's parents 'buy' the bride, and she becomes part of their family.

"For most women there is no easy way out of an unhappy marriage.

"Divorce would mean leaving behind the financial security of the family, casting them into an uncertain future.

"Women will face an even more terrible future in 20 years time. Abduction and trafficking of women will increase. So will prostitution, as well as sexual violence against women and rape."

The program noted that migration to the city was even more bleak than the government wanted to admit.

"In the manufacturing hubs of the south-east coastal provinces, up to 70% of the millions of migrant workers are women, mostly in their teens and 20s.

"The move to the city is not without risk. Many young women have been sexually abused by their bosses, and working conditions are often abysmal.

Needless to say, the treatment of women in China is still eons away from what the communist government would have the outside world believe." [2]

SOURCE:

[1] Allen, Christopher, *Traditions Weigh on Chinese Women*

[2] *"China: Women of the Country,"* was broadcast on Tuesday, 20 June, 2006 at 21:00 BST on BBC Two. Much of this information for this article was taken from this broadcast.

Article 51.

"The exercise by citizens of the People's Republic of China of their freedoms and rights may not infringe upon the interests of the *state*..."

If there ever was a law regarding the superiority of the state over the individual, Article 51 is it. All one has to do is consider the phrase "interests of the state." Again these interests are intentionally not defined—thus granting extreme latitude to those who wield power in the current communist Chinese infrastructure.

Article 56.

"It is the duty of citizens of the People's Republic of China to pay taxes in accordance with the law."

It has been estimated that 70 to 90 percent of Chinese people either knowingly cheat on their taxes—or pay no taxes at all. Ironically, those who do pay are the ones employed by the state, but in actuality they are simply paying into their own *guaranteed lifetime* retirement system.

There is even money that is commonly referred to as "grey money" in which huge amounts of undeclared revenue is routinely not paid by citizens. These amounts are so enormous, with virtually no way of accounting, that the government simply pretends that this phenomenon doesn't exist.

CHAPTER III. THE STRUCTURE OF THE STATE

Section 1. The National People's Congress

Article 57.

"The National People's Congress of the People's Republic of China is the highest organ of *state* power. Its permanent body is the Standing Committee of the National People's Congress."

Section 2. The President of the People's Republic of China

Article 79.

"The President and Vice-President of the People's Republic of China are elected by the National People's Congress. Citizens of the People's Republic of China who have the right to vote and to stand for election and who have reached the age of 45 are eligible for election as President or Vice-President of the People's Republic of China. The term of office of the President and Vice-President of the People's Republic of China is the same as that of the National People's Congress, and they shall serve no more than two consecutive terms."

The phrase "who have the right to vote" is key here. Throughout my stay in China I never met anyone who voted for any politician in high office. This is one of the most convoluted definitions of democratic voting in the world. It is nothing more than a *selection* process—not an election in any democratic sense of the word.

Section 3. The State Council

Article 85.

"The *State* Council, that is, the Central People's Government of the People's Republic of China, is the executive body of the highest organ of *state* power; it is the highest organ of *state* administration."

Article 86.

"The *State* Council is composed of the following: The Premier; The Vice-Premiers; The *State* Councillors; The Ministers in charge of Ministries; The Ministers in charge of Commissions; The Auditor-General; and The Secretary-General. The Premier has overall responsibility for the *State* Council. The Ministers have overall responsibility for the respective ministries or commissions under their charge. The organization of the *State* Council is prescribed by law."

In a nutshell, none of these positions are filled by direct vote of the people. They are picked by the politicians themselves while all the time appearing to the international community that they are actually democratic in fashion and representing the will of the so-called masses.

As of this writing there are four amendments to the constitution of the People's Republic of China.

NOTE: It should be pointed out that when looking at the constitution of the People's Republic of China, there tends to be different interpretations due to the various English translations that are available. However, they all tend to say basically the same thing even though the actual words may, in some renderings, differ slightly.

SOURCES:

http://english.people.com.cn/constitution/constitution.html
http://www.usconstitution.net/china.html

A CLOSER LOOK AT THE CHINESE COMMUNIST FLAG

Article 136.

The Chinese flag, Five-Starred Red Flag (Wu Xing Hong Qi) basically stands for the following:

The red represents the blood of all soldiers lost in war.

There is one large yellow star with four smaller yellow stars, all located in the upper left hand corner.

The four smaller stars represent the four revolutionary classes:

The worker
The farmer
The student
The soldier

There is also another explanation that designates the four smaller stars as representing the following classes of Chinese society:

The workers
The peasants
The petty bourgeoisie
The patriotic capitalists

But in both interpretations there is no dispute as to what the largest yellow star in the middle represents—and it is *not* China as a nation.

The biggest star on the People's Republic of China's national flag symbolizes the unequivocal consolidation of power solely in the hands of the *Chinese Communist Party*.

If it really were the *People's* Republic, then it seems to me that the people would be the main thrust of concern. If this were the case then there would be no need to make the Chinese Communist Party the central focus of their national flag.

But the Chinese people don't seem to even consider this idea—and for good reason. Anyone who speaks out against the Chinese Communist Party is, according to the constitution, automatically guilty of treason because they are actually speaking against the main emphasis of the flag itself. All who speak out against the "party" in such fashion are summarily silenced—in many cases permanently.

So, if you are against the Chinese Communist Party you are automatically against China. It's a brilliant play on mind control that the Chinese people themselves still do not fully appreciate.

As a bit of trivia, the flag was first raised by Mao Zedong in Tiananmen Square in 1949, thus adding special significance to its elevated stature in the hierarchy of the "New" China of today.

SOURCE:

Wikipedia, The Free Encyclopedia, Internet source:
http://en.wikipedia.org/wiki/Flag_of_the_People%27s_Republic_of_China

CHAPTER 2

WHEN THE INTERNATIONAL DECEPTION STARTED IN EARNEST

Globalization

Many countries and organizations will be held accountable in the years to come—especially the four inter-related international bodies known as the World Bank, the International Monetary Fund (IMF), the World Trade Organization (WTO) and the United Nations (UN)—when the present status quo in the "New" China finally breaks down. When this happens there will be disastrous consequences, not only for the Asian region, but for the world as a whole.

The recent, sudden downturn in the Chinese stock market in February 2007—where a one day decline was the largest in a decade, was brought about by rumors that the communist government was considering a capital gains tax on equities to stem inflation and curb the ever-increasing spiral of real estate speculation—produced a run on the Chinese stock exchange, sending economic shock waves around the world. Government officials quickly came out and stated that they were not going to raise taxes on capital gains after all.

This one event shows, in dramatic fashion, how vulnerable the Chinese government is to economic upheaval.

With that in mind, these four official bodies are nothing more than fronts for the misguided concept most often referred to as

"Globalization." No matter how hard mega-corporations protest, they are working hand in glove with the communist government for the benefit of themselves to effectively subjugate the Chinese working masses to the lowest level of human decency and dignity for the mere sake of astronomical profits with little or no concern for the poor and powerless who literally give their lives working just to survive.

The World Bank and the International Monetary Fund (IMF)

In 1990, China was admitted into the World Bank. Add to this the fact that China is a member of the IMF. These were the first steps in currying international favor in China's direction—for the explicit purpose of legalized banditry of hundreds of millions of migrant workers at a fraction of the world labor cost, in the name of Globalization.

International consortiums, mega-industrial corporations and multi-billion dollar private investment firms are working in a concerted effort with these two organizations to secure their share of the financial exploitation of the vast Chinese labor market and the literal hundreds of billions of dollars it is capable of squeezing out of them.

Through fear, intimidation, and threat of physical violence coupled with insurmountable graft, corruption and naked greed they go about their business of implementing a systematic, modern day, globalized slave labor force for the benefit of the few, at the expense of the many.

The World Trade Organization (WTO)

In 2001, China was "invited" to join the WTO to the sheer delight of mega-corporate international conglomerates. They all see this as a very positive development to implement their long-range plans of securing the mass-production facilities of the vast Chinese labor force without having to pay for even basic minimum worker's compensation, rudimentary health care or any other benefits that advanced economies are required, by law, to provide for their employees.

ADMISSION TO THE UNITED NATIONS HUMAN RIGHTS COUNCIL

As recently as 19 June 2006, China—as a *communist* country—was awarded a seat on the UN Human Rights Council for *three* years. India, on the other hand, a *democracy*, was also admitted—but only for *one* year.

Why Such a Discrepancy?

India is a democracy—and therefore the possibility of total *mind control* and *human rights abuses* are not as easy to accomplish as they are in China. Plus, to the horror of most international corporate conglomerates, India's legal system is founded on British Common Law—a situation that is almost never alluded to in the mainstream mass media for obvious reasons.

China has no such basis for law and therefore pretty much does as it pleases in the way of awarding contracts, setting up rules of negoti-ation, agreements on bribes and under-the-table considerations, not to mention little or no enforcement of human rights or the working conditions of the exploited poor.

Another reason why China was chosen over India is the fact that English comprehension is not as widespread in China as it is in India. Whereas many Indians can voice their complaints in the international language of English, Chinese people are not so fortunate, as yet, with their English linguistic ability. Consequently, many Chinese dissi-dents must rely on translators to get their point across to the outside world. China was therefore a much better choice simply because the "peasants" can't speak English.

At the root of this *mind control* and *human rights abuses* lies the perennial bottom line—unimaginable corporate wealth.

While international corporations piously proclaim to be "providing jobs for the masses," they conveniently look the other way when it comes to the deplorable working conditions, scant health and safety standards and abhorrently inhumane treatment that the unfortunate migrant and labor classes are compelled to work under, on a daily basis, or be fired on the spot if they even breathe a word of discontent.

People have to eat. Hunger is the biggest suppressor of the human spirit—for without food—liberty and individual freedom are literally starved to death.

It is not hard to figure out why, after nearly 60 years of Dynastic Communist Dictatorship, that China still has 1,000,000,000 people living at, or below, the poverty line.

Keep them there, keep them just barely alive, work them until they die, then replace them with someone else. This is the true unspoken mantra of the Chinese Communist Party.

Business conglomerates will deny this, right along with their communist counterparts, and say that 300 million have been lifted out of poverty and more are to follow. But the masses will *not* be allowed to follow, for once they become middle class who will then be the labor force to supply the ever-increasing worldwide demand for cheaper and cheaper Chinese goods?

But Are So Many People Really That Poor?

According to recent economic research, the Gini coefficient is the rule of thumb as a widely accepted measuring device that depicts or demonstrates the inequality between the rich and the poor, where zero (0) means complete equality and one (1) equals total inequality.

Recently, China has exceeded the 0.4 mark. This is considered to be the international number in which a potentially dangerous situation could arise.

This measure is used in most countries throughout the world to show the economic discrepancies between those who have a lot and those who have little or nothing.

But the word "poverty" has become so sanitized nowadays by a plethora of Non-governmental agencies (NGOs)—and their professional lobbyists that support these *profit making enterprises* and receive exorbitant fees in the process—that poverty has lost its original meaning.

I choose to call poverty in China what it really is. Pure, unadulterated, human squalor.

In an article in the Shanghai Daily dated, Thursday 20, October 2005, Paul Wolfowitz, president of the World Bank, stated that, "In Heping Village in Gansu province, some people just recently moved out of *caves*."

Bear in mind, this is the 21st century.

What About Their Vaunted Personal Savings Rate?

By the end of 2005, Chinese families had accrued a record US $1.7 *trillion* dollars in personal savings. This sounds like a huge amount, until you consider a few other statistics well hidden from public scrutiny by the government-controlled mass media.

Roughly 6% of the population owns approximately 65% of the total wealth in China—the government controls the rest.

When people read that the average income of Chinese people, according to 2005 estimates, was $6,800 per capita, it sounds very encouraging. But when you consider that 1,000,000,000 people make no where near that amount—in their *lifetime*—it loses all credibility.

If one person has 10 million dollars and nine other people have nothing, according to this method of calculation, then all 10 would theoretically be classified as millionaires. It is a shrewd numbers game that is trotted out all the time to justify an unjustifiable situation.

With convoluted statistics to make their case, these international bodies tend to adhere to an unwritten code of *moral ambiguity* when it comes to China in particular.

They act in complicit silence, in fully agreed upon deference, to the exorbitant amount of potential profit that is to be realized— under the accepted rules of a completely totalitarian communist dictatorship—all the while turning a benign eye to the obvious plight of the "common people" forced to subsist under such appalling conditions of internationally calculated squalor.

And therein lies the reason why India, as a democracy, was given one year, while China was handed a three year membership on the UN Human Rights Commission. If it were not so perversely obscene it would make for supreme black comedy. Sad to say, the Chinese people are not laughing.

When the next revolution comes—and come it will—these same international bodies will have to pay an extremely high price as compensation to the people of China for their exponential greed that they are now unabashedly demonstrating to the world—in the name of Globalization.

CHAPTER 3

...a Dynasty found, the people live a pitiful life,
a Dynasty lost, the people live a pitiful life...

Two lines from the poem entitled, Tong Guan
(Recall History in Tong Guan), written by
Chinese poet, Zhang Hao, A.D. 1270–1329

A Chinese student of mine, and very good friend, brought the above poem to my attention and specifically noted these two lines, which, in their brevity, encompass 5,000 years of Chinese history.

FIRST AND FOREMOST: CONTROL THE PEOPLE

The Cycle of Dynasties

How can a nation such as China, with its long history and a population of 1.3 billion people still be a developing country?

Basically, the answer lies in China's natural—*historical*—abhorrence to share power. So, instead of the country's progress gradually going up, as most other countries do—China simply keeps going in a circle.

This *Cycle of Dynasties* usually lasts between 50 to 100 years, on average, and for the most part consists of a complete revolution, mass killings of the deposed status quo, disavowing all rules and regulations and starting all over again—with another group of malcontents in power.

There is not one revolution in Chinese history where the plight of the common peasant has been bettered. It simply stays the same—miserable—just as those lines written over 700 years ago so poignantly attest to.

THE TRIANGLE OF TYRANNICAL CONTROL

The Chinese Communist Party (CCP)

At the top of this Triangle of Tyrannical Control is the Chinese Communist Party.

Graft and corruption are so conspicuous that many government employees, be they national, provisional or municipal workers, don't even do the basic rudiments of their job without illegal monetary compensation. This is how things get done in today's "New" China.

Some of the Many Benefits of Working for the Communist Chinese Party—from the National to the Municipal Level

Each person in state-run enterprises, government organizations and communist party organizations receive:

1. Worker compensation for injury.
2. Time off for sick leave.
3. Maternity benefits and time off from work.
4. Disability benefits—for life.
5. Complete retirement benefits covering both medical and dental expenditures—for life.
6. Survivor pensions—for life.

The Chinese Military

The second point of control is the Chinese Military. The cadre is well-disciplined and ruthless when it comes to carrying out its duties to suppress the people wherever and whenever they try to complain or actually get out of control.

Some human rights groups estimate that over 30,000 protests took place in 2005 in locales far away from city centers—a great many of which turned into all-out riots—but simply have not been reported by the government controlled media. This will be disputed by every high-level government official. But it still remains the truth.

During the Tiananmen Square Massacre, the local military actually refused to fire on their own people and regular army troops had to be called in from the outlying areas to put down the rebellion. They did not hesitate to murder hundreds of students. Had they refused, they would have been jailed—as were many of the soldiers that declined to shoot the students in the first place.

To this day the outside world is unaware as to how close China came to all-out revolution in 1989. The ruling status quo does not intend to let that happen again—under any circumstances.

During the Fuzhou floods of September 2005, some of the worst in the last 100 years, I ventured downtown to check out the severity of the storm and the resultant damage that it had inflicted on the people. It was devastating to say the least. Businesses completely submerged, houses flooded, everywhere quiet desperation.

But what really caught my attention were the truckloads of Chinese military personnel riding around in troop carriers, 20 or more soldiers in the back, fatigues starched, helmets shining, boots expertly polished—and not one soldier getting out to lend a hand. They were there to make sure that the people didn't go on a rampage in utter frustration. The military trucks drove around all day long—and I saw not one soldier actually help anybody.

The Chinese Police

This is the local strong-arm of the controlling faction of the Chinese Communist Party—more often than not in concert with local organized crime syndicates (Chinese Triad). They keep a lid on things as best they can. They are on the front lines every day, interacting with the people trying to placate a perennially volatile situation.

People call the police only as a last resort. They know once the police are called in, then the bureaucracy sets itself in motion. This means mounds of paperwork, endless trips to the local police station and in many cases, bribes paid to get results.

Bluntly stated, Chinese people don't trust the police and abhor getting them involved unless the crime is too heinous for them to be excluded.

In the final analysis, the police are not charged with enforcing the law. Their main function is to simply *maintain the peace.*

"I Didn't See a Thing"

This phrase is programmed into the hearts and minds of every Chinese citizen.

Members of the Chinese Military routinely use government vehicles to do their shopping, drive their kids to private schools and ferry their wives to the beauty parlor—all at public expense. But absolutely nobody complains—and if they do, they do not complain for long.

All military and government vehicles are allowed through toll roads without paying the designated fee—even though many of the excursions are for personal matters.

Military officers, civil servants and other dignitaries many times take government four-wheel-drive vehicles on vacation, write off the gas expenses to "official business" and nobody is any the wiser. Again, nobody dares to complain—if they know what is good for them.

"I didn't see at thing" is now the accepted norm in today's "New China."

The Frightening Efficiency of the Triangular Structure

Notice the way this structure is assembled. The Chinese Communist Party (the all-encompassing governmental octopus) is at the top. They run the whole country from the political sense of the word and have supreme, unquestioned authority as to what is legal and what is not to be tolerated.

The Chinese Military establishment is at the left base while the Chinese Police complete the physical incarceration at the right base of the triangle.

The military and police, along with noted criminal entities, are the main elements that have all the firepower—*the guns*—to enforce the will of the Chinese Communist Party. Make no mistake about it. The Chinese Communist Party enforces *its* will, not the will of the people.

Throughout history, despotic rulers, have always disarmed the populace.

Joseph Stalin outlawed private weapons then murdered 26 million. This is the main reason why Russian civilians fought the Nazis with sickles and pitchforks. Stalin had taken all their guns.

Adolph Hitler made it a point to confiscate all private weapons as soon as he became dictator, effectively leaving the people defenseless. He then proceeded to start World War II.

And the same goes for China. The people have been literally stripped of all physical means with which to resist the tyrannical rule of the Chinese Communist Party. So they have no other choice but to meekly fall into lockstep and do as they are told—for the time being.

The Invisible "Fourth" Leg to the Chinese Triangle of Tyrannical Control—Mother Nature

In actuality, this is what the Chinese status quo is most uncertain about simply because they know they can't control it. Every time a huge natural disaster strikes, the first thing the government does is roll out the military, have them take a few photo ops for the government controlled media—and the gullible international press— then pack up and go back to their barracks. More than once have vast areas been completely sealed off from any outside "interference" or observation, once disaster has struck.

Sometimes months go by before the government actually takes decisive action and many times it does nothing at all. It is one of the most subtle ways the government can keep its burgeoning population in check and save money at the same time—especially if the town or province is poor or has not been behaving in the "proper manner."

The people of Lanping Village, in the eastern province of Zhejiang, in August, 2006, suffered the devastation of the strongest typhoon in half a century when Typhoon Saomai decimated the village.

The following is a direct quote from an Internet article written by columnist, Ben Blanchard, covering the disaster.

"I heard hundreds died. The government has shut off villages where the death toll is really high to stop news getting out," said a Chinese

48

youth who would not give his name.

Mr. Blanchard continues by saying, "The communist government, determined to maintain stability at all costs, has a habit of covering up bad news, although disaster death tolls are no longer supposed to be state secrets.

"Mistrust of the government is common in Zhejiang, which is far from the capital and where a strong entrepreneurial spirit has bred a flourishing private sector."

And this is only a fraction of the news that is getting out albeit via the Internet. Every town and village in China has its own story of how the government has either been late in reacting to natural disasters, or has simply not acted at all, leaving the people to fend for themselves the best they can.

These are not isolated incidences. They happen on a daily basis.

"People First" (Yi Ren Wei Ben)

This is the new rallying cry of the Chinese Communist Party that the "People" are first.

As shown from the previous brief description of Chinese history, it has been awash in blood from the very beginning. Deception, corruption, murder and greed are paramount factors throughout the long succession of Chinese Dynasties. And the Communist Dynasty is no different.

So, instead of reporting the truth, the mass-media is trying to *sell the idea*—in full tandem with the Chinese Communist Party (which, according to the constitution, totally controls the media)— of a "New" China in which everything has now changed for the benefit of the people.

This is a finely tuned lie of enormous proportion. For if the People's Republic of China was really for the people, as it proclaims to be, then there would be no need to make a declaration of "The People First"—in the first place.

"Premier Pledges Prosperity For All"

This headline news on the front page of the Monday, March 6, 2006 edition of the China Daily, shows how determined, and scared, the ruling Chinese Communist Dynasty really is.

These proclamations have been made before with the same end result. The ugly truth is, over three quarters of the Chinese population is still subsisting at, or below, the poverty level.

The Chinese communists came to power on October 1, 1949, pushed the Kuomingtang off the mainland and onto the Island of Formosa, now Taiwan. While the mainland wallowed in one internal squabble after another, the Island of Taiwan flourished, so much so that it is referred to as one of the "Four Asian Tigers," the other three being, Singapore, Hong Kong and South Korea.

Yet, almost 60 years after the fact, Mainland China is still a developing nation. In effect, China has always been a developing nation, simply because of its traditional refusal to substantially help the poor. Instead, throughout history, each successive dynasty has opted to "control" the masses, instead of trusting and helping them.

The beautiful castles, the ever-enchanting Great Wall—right down to the most revered Forbidden City—are all products of a feudal (slave) society. Hundreds of thousands of peasants died as forced laborers during construction of the Great Wall.

Most Chinese take immense pride in the Forbidden City (so much so, that the government recently kicked Starbucks out because it wasn't Chinese enough), but completely lose sight of the fact that it too was built by feudal peasants, thousands of whom died in the process. Remarkably beautiful, yes. But it still remained, for centuries, forbidden to all but the most prestigious, powerful and wealthy.

So where does that leave the people of the "New" China? Simply put, trapped inside this tyrannically triangle—trying to get out.

In essence, all Chinese are under virtual martial law.

BASIC OVERALL ANALYSIS OF FREEDOM IN CHINA

Freedom in the World 2005

"Since 1978, Freedom House has published Freedom in the World, an annual comparative assessment of the state of political rights and civil liberties around the world.

"The survey finds that 49 countries are not free. The 2.4 billion inhabitants (37%) of these countries, nearly three-fifths of whom live in China, are denied most basic political rights and civil liberties.

"The scale is on a ranking of 1 (most free) to 7 (least free).

"China ranks 6.5, along with Belarus, Equatorial Guinea, Eritrea, Haiti, Laos, Somalia, Uzbekistan, Vietnam and Zimbabwe."

SOURCE:

Direct quotes from *Freedom in the World*, 2005, published by Freedom House. http://www.freedomhouse.or/research/survey2005.htm

CHAPTER 4

THE BEGINNING OF THE SYSTEMATIC GOVERNMENTAL ABANDONMENT OF THE PEOPLE BY THE CHINESE COMMUNIST PARTY

No More Free Education

Control the mind—control the person. As pointed out earlier in the Chinese constitution the government controls all elements of education. Children are required to attend mandatory schooling, for which their parents contribute a large part of their income, yet are still forced to adhere to the institutional teaching that is imposed upon them. They have no other choice. Home schooling is against the law.

The canceling of totally free education is one of the most exasperating developments for the people of China. In reality, if you don't have enough money to attend school, you don't go. This holds true, especially for females. First the boy goes to school. Then, if there is any money left over, the girl can attend.

Families now regularly go deep into debt to pay for schooling that was once completely free. Houses are borrowed against, both parents are working longer and harder just to keep up with the ever increasing cost of education, while at the same time educational competition becomes even more stifling.

Communist Party Recruiting

Since the communist government still controls the people with an iron fist, they are constantly recruiting children that appear to be "appropriate" to someday becoming a member of the party— thus pitting students against each other at a very early age.

Pupils that are judged in a favorable light by their teachers are appointed as class monitors and subtly learn the intricacies of reporting on other students' "inappropriate" behavior. If they are deemed well-suited in this endeavor, they are recommended by their teacher to the proper authorities and are followed throughout their educational career.

If they continue to act in the proper manner, they are approached, usually during their first year in university, to join the CCP— thus securing a promise of lifetime employment before they even graduate.

This is the secret dream of many students, a ticket to security and relative success, as long as they toe the Chinese Communist Party line, for the rest of their lives.

Forced Education

You teach a person through logical thinking. This leads to questioning the status quo, its claim to legitimacy and eventually challenging rules that are unethical or illegal. This type of "liberal" education traditionally leads to the concept of freedom in the most general sense of the word.

You teach a person—you train a dog. You don't use reason with a dog. You don't try to explain what to do in certain circumstances. You don't point out logical conclusions.

A dog is trained by forced, rote command, with an immediate reward when the task is accomplished in the appropriate fashion. When something is done wrong you punish the dog and no reward is given.

To program, or indoctrinate a person, you use logic based on assumptions that are crafted to your desired goals and objectives, couched in a permanent pattern of training.

Questions—are out of the question.

You train with authority, allow no deviation from the stated program and accept nothing short of trained perfection.

To program, to indoctrinate, thus, is education, communist Chinese style.

Stroke Order Way of Life

I can think of no other way to illustrate this point than the monumental task of learning the Chinese writing system. It takes years of tedious, rote memorization just to get the basics down. There are appropriate stroke orders, stylized methods of writing and boundaries to be adhered to. If the stroke order is wrong, even if the final written character is OK, it is considered incorrect by the teacher and the student has to do it over—according to the properly accepted stroke order.

If the Chinese character is written correctly, but outside the prescribed boundary, then it is still considered wrong and the student is made to repeat the task yet again.

The Chinese writing system is one of the most ingenious devices ever conjured up by man to keep the masses—who for centuries couldn't even read or write—in their place, learn the function of rote memory, not question authority and stay within ones social boundaries at all times.

In a sense, the Chinese stroke order of life, in conjunction with rote memorization has kept the masses under control, except when they get frustrated to the point of "glorious revolution" and everything is turned upside down and they start all over again.

From the outset, learning in China is not fun. It is hard labor and with the attachment of "academic endeavor" provided as additional proof, the subtle message to all Chinese people being—learn by rote, don't question, do as you are told—and be thankful for your lot in life.

Chinese people are by no means born stupid. They are just trained stupid.

Indoctrination v. Education

The Chinese education system is in no way whatsoever interested in giving their young people a comprehensive education in the truest sense of the word.

The public education system is the cornerstone, the driving force, the social mechanism that relentlessly enforces the subtle, systematic feudalism that permeates each and every aspect of Chinese life.

Keeping students ignorant of their country's past mistakes ensures the cadre in command that they can control the actions, thoughts, words and deeds of every charge entrusted to them.

Spontaneous thinking and logical reasoning are systematically suppressed in Chinese schools throughout the country.

Classes are held on the history of China and how it was always at the mercy of foreigners and, in most cases, laying the blame for China's present state of affairs at the feet of the rest of the world.

This historical concept has an element of truth in it. But what is not accurate is how the students are indoctrinated about how the "glorious" CCP has brought China to where it is today.

No mention of the millions of people that died because of the government's ill-advised forays into backyard steel production. It is merely referred to as a "mistake" and conveniently swept under China's vast, historical rug.

Most students nowadays have no historical perspective as to what happened at Tiananmen Square in 1989. Many of my well-meaning university students actually took me to task when I questioned them about it. Only after lengthy discussions was I able to get them to consider that it even took place. But once I began to show them the information—on *English language* websites—they started to understand the true implications of that period of history.

After much discussion one of my best students came up to me after class and told me how ashamed he was for not knowing his own country's past. It was the first time he had ever learned that students were actually murdered by their own soldiers—just for demanding democracy in China.

But I misunderstood his feelings because when I told him it was all right, and that now he actually was aware of what happened, he countered by saying, "Oh, I am not ashamed about not knowing the truth regarding Tiananmen Square. I am ashamed because I learned it from a foreigner."

In China, *Face*, and all its dire consequences, tends to raise its ugly head at the most unexpected times.

Rote Memory

Rote memory is the norm in the Chinese education system. Students are given lists, tables, study charts, books and told to memorize them.

The concept of give and take in the classroom is not nearly as open as it is in the West and the idea of "free discussion" is extremely limited if not altogether suppressed.

Selective Learning v. Comprehensive Learning

The Chinese Communist Party is very adept at teaching history that is to their advantage. All countries do this to a large degree but China tends to carry it to extremes. In many instances historical fact is bent out of shape to such an extent that it is unrecognizable.

Sometimes it is completely reshaped or, in the extreme, entirely deleted from textbooks altogether.

In this sense the government is again very much akin to its Japanese cousins in tainting history to meet their own needs and desired ends.

Copy-Thought Process as Opposed to Creative-Thought Process

A large portion of university students cheat in some form or another on their term papers, quizzes, tests, or final examinations. Granted, it is a matter of survival but it is also a matter of cultural heritage.

For centuries, apprentices were instructed to copy their master's style in every detail to save the art and the art form, thus passing it from generation to generation.

For example, an artisan would study for years, trying to duplicate every aspect of his master's technique. When the examiners could no longer tell the apprentice's work from that of the master the student was then considered a master in his own right, and awarded his *Master's* degree.

It is this type of thinking that still pervades the so-called academic climate in Chinese colleges and universities, and if not curtailed will be a major stumbling block to the future progress of China in the years to come.

However, it is still very difficult to throw off this inherent cultural trait. Since the pressure is so intense to pass life-defining college entrance exams, cheating is still a widespread phenomenon in China.

Yet, the communist government is so fearful of developing a *creative-thought process* as opposed to a *copy-thought process*, that they simply refuse to allow the idea of free thinking to take root in the university system. This is the main reason why so many highly acclaimed academics leave China to conduct further study in other countries— and choose never to return again to their homeland.

Pressure-Cooker College Entrance Exams

In 2006, 9.6 *million* students sat for national college entrance examinations. That is more than twice the entire population of New Zealand.

In China, tests are the ultimate decisive factor in determining a person's course in life. The competition is so intense that it is difficult to describe in words. You actually have to see it to believe it. In many instances, it is a matter of life and death, for the outcome of these excruciating examinations literally set the foundation for the rest of the student's existence on earth.

Statistics point to an alarming rate of depression during this time of year. Yet, the government will not admit that depression is even a factor, so great is the shame of mental illness in China.

Face simply will not allow the CCP to admit to any sort of mental disorder whatsoever.

Parents and Students on Oxygen

Every year during college entrance exam time, students and their parents are extremely stressed throughout the whole process. Large numbers of parents go so far as to rent a hotel room a week before the exam period, thus ensuring a private place to cram for the upcoming tests. Many parents physically stay with their children, making sure that they study the required 10 to 15 hours a day before the crucial examination period begins.

At break times during the testing period many students actually inhale pure oxygen. Others take sleep deprivation tablets (coffee stimulates the bladder and is thus not recommended), for once you are in the examination room, and the ID cards and pictures physically checked and a seat assigned, no student is allowed to leave for any reason whatsoever. If you do go outside it is an automatic failure for the whole entrance examination period and you must start it all over again—next year.

During the extended examination time, which lasts for approximately three days, both the students and parents have been known to have nervous breakdowns, erupt in fits of rage and engage in other forms of anti-social behavior.

No Menstrual Cycle—Period!

The absurdity to which all this educational hysteria has reached its peak seems to lie with female students in particular.

No matter what the Chinese constitution says about gender equality, it simply isn't true. Girls are not treated equally, especially when it comes to educational endeavors. Their choices of life careers are severely limited according to Chinese mores and those female students who are fortunate enough to attend school are under even more intense pressure to succeed.

A recent study found girls in remote areas to be dropping out of school at a faster rate than previously assumed. It is surmised that since they are girls they don't need an education as much as boys do—because males are still traditionally considered the breadwinners in the family.

Therefore, it is not uncommon to observe a high school girl going into the local pharmacy, accompanied by her mother, to get contraceptive pills. This is not done because the girl is promiscuous or wants to have intercourse without getting pregnant. It is done to prolong the girl's menstrual cycle—putting it off until the college entrance examination is over.

I was personally informed by one school counselor that she actually advises female students of this procedure to ensure that "nothing goes wrong" during the scheduled testing time.

Suicide—As a Way of Life

From a very early age Chinese children are forced to study academic subjects at a dizzying rate. Due to the extreme amount of competition, a growing amount of toddlers start their academic career at 5:30 A.M., go to a private pre-school, graduate to elementary school, progressing on to middle, then high school, all the while studying, on average, 10–12 hours a day.

Then the pace starts to pick up with the college entrance exams and the extreme pressure kids are put under to "do your best for yourself and the family name."

The need to succeed at all costs is getting more and more difficult for students to endure, with an increasing number opting for suicide. It is a growing problem that has gained some national attention but has produced very little in curbing this widespread phenomenon.

One roadblock is the social stigma attached to psychiatry in general. No one wants to have a "nut" in the family. It does not bode well for communal relations and is like the plague when it comes time to get married. Any record—or *rumor*—of psychological dysfunction and a person is stigmatized for life. This feeling is so prevalent in China that mental disorder is many times referred to as a "Western" disease, making it totally *foreign* to the Chinese way of thinking.

Here again, *Face* is the guiding light. It is very difficult to get verifiable statistics on this grim reality but a growing number of students kill themselves every year during the college entrance exam period.

The shame of failing is so extreme that I had pupils tell me that, in some cases, it is better for a student to kill himself rather than bring shame upon themselves and their family if they don't perform up to the prescribed standards.

The pressure is even heavier on students that come from rural villages who were chosen by their neighbors to receive communal financial aid with which to go to college, graduate and bring wealth and prosperity back to their village as return payment for being subsidized with community funding.

Pressure on these students will only increase as the intensity to gain educational advantage continues to mount.

Such is daily life in the Chinese academic pressure-cooker that now exists.

And statistics such as the one where 3,000,000 college graduates were unable to land a job in 2005 don't help matters any. A disproportionate number of university graduates are now driving taxis, working in restaurants, doing menial labor—or simply unemployed.

Yet Not One Noble Prize Winner

It is astounding to consider the simple fact that not one Chinese person—working and living in China—has ever won a Noble Prize. Out of a population of 1.3 billion people this is simply an incredible statistic. Yet it shows how perverse the concept of mind-control continues to be in China.

However, I do not see this situation continuing for much longer. China's international *Face* will, sooner or later, have to allow some of its citizens to compete on an equal footing with their academic counterparts around the globe.

It is also a very embarrassing position for China to be in and one that is under discussion as I write. There are even rumors that "monetary considerations might be in order" to speed up the process of a Chinese academic finally being considered to receive a Nobel Prize.

The first Chinese person to actually win will be touted as a national hero, wined and dined all over the country and be the most sought after talk show guest in the nation.

The government might even stipulate a special holiday and present the recipient with a national medal of the highest honor.

But first, the government has to relax its penchant to control every aspect of the educational process in China.

Not until then will a *bona fide* Noble Prize candidate emerge from the educational straightjacket that China is now suffocating under.

Student Riots—Rarely Reported—No Domino Effect Wanted

A tremendous amount of campus unrest goes unreported in China. Students want to change the present status quo but are thwarted at every juncture by local police and, in extreme cases, the military.

The West doesn't have the slightest idea as to how much student unrest there is in China. The stories that do manage to get out usually are the result of Internet usage, thus the government's determination to control its dissemination of information as much as possible.

In an article entitled, *Chinese Riot Over World Cup Power Cuts*, by Christopher Bodeen, of the Associated Press and downloaded from the Internet, he states that, "Campus unrest is treated with extreme sensitivity in China following the 1989 student pro-democracy protests that led to the bloody military crackdown in Beijing's Tiananmen Square."

In the same article he talks about another school that went on a rampage then added that, "Police and local government and education officials have refused to comment on the Shengda protests, believed to be among the worst episodes of campus violence in recent years." He goes on to say that, "Both incidents were also not reported in the official state media."

This report was e-mailed to Mr. Bodeen by a Chinese student via the Internet—an action that can land a person in jail for many years in today's "New" China.

SOURCE:

http://medianet.qianlong.com/7692/2006/06/27/2623@3268575.htm

CHAPTER 5

THE CONTINUATION OF THE GOVERNMENTAL ABANDONMENT OF THE PEOPLE

No More Free Health or Dental Care

No more free healthcare or dental care is one of the biggest gripes that the people have with regard to the direction the government is going as of late.

I had the unfortunate opportunity of visiting two different hospitals in China and was astounded at what took place. The teacher that I was accompanying was treated like royalty, ushered in ahead of a long line of people and the financial papers filled out on the spot as to his ability to pay.

The cost for medical help was totally out of proportion compared to the average wage of Chinese workers, but that is not what bothered me. What really drove the point home was how much money they could milk out of "rich" foreigners, at the expense of taking care of other people who seemed to need it even more than my teacher friend. While people were lying on the floor in obvious pain the hospital staff hastened to literally step over them to get to my colleague and take care of him first—not out of compassion but out of sheer, monetary greed.

To top it all off, he was escorted to a section of the hospital, reserved for foreigners and other "dignitaries," and treated to a private room with color TV and a king size bed. Needless to say, the bill for all this "medical" treatment was king size to boot.

But for the general populace, free medical care is a thing of the past. What people are now forced to do is purchase healthcare insurance and pay for their own hospital and dental expenses—much to the delight of international insurance giants from around the world—and to the consternation of every Chinese person that I spoke with.

Coming Health Disaster #1—The Elderly

As stated a number of times before, China's population is approximately 1.3 billion. The "point" 3 is somewhat misleading at first glance. That decimal figure roughly equates to the population of the USA—300 million people. Then you add 1,000,000,000 more citizens on top of that and you start to realize the magnitude of China's historical population problem.

According to an article in the China Daily, "The number of elderly people in China, above the age of 60, is expected to reach 243 million by 2020." That's a tremendous amount of old folks.

If this is true, the outlook for China's ability to take care of its aging population is simply untenable.

Coming Health Disaster #2—HIV/AIDS

According to another article in the China Daily, "Official statistics show that among China's 840,000 people living with HIV/AIDS, 45% get infected through drug injection, 25% through blood transfusions and 30% through unsafe sex, a factor which has been steadily rising."

If the propaganda angle of the Chinese Communist Party is to be taken into account, I would very much suspect that these numbers are on the extreme low end of the scale. I would hazard a guess that the numbers are much higher—and rising at an unprecedented and purposefully—undocumented rate.

In China, sexually transmitted diseases (STDs), are a serious social taboo—especially for females, because they are labeled as "loose women" and automatically disqualified for marriage. Young girls who are found to have HIV or worse yet, AIDS, are banned from their villages, drift towards the urban areas and end up in prostitution—more often than not participating in endless acts of unprotected sex.

HIV and AIDS are at epidemic proportions—but since there is such a lack of evidence from people willing to come forth for fear of social ostracism—the extent of the real dangers associated with HIV and AIDS are not statistically verifiable.

The Chinese government has a very curious attitude toward HIV and AIDS. Formally, they decry it and are doing "everything in their power to eradicate this scourge from the face of the earth."

But in private they actually feel that those who contract HIV or AIDS, "probably did something wrong to get the disease in the first place, so this is their punishment." I actually had a professor divulge this opinion to me after he was well on his way to drinking himself into oblivion. But he meant every word of it.

Another, even darker proposition, is that HIV and AIDS are just two more "natural" methods employed by the government to keep a cap on the population growth in general.

Coming Health Disaster #3—Up in Smoke

It is not uncommon to see people lighting up in restaurants and bars. It happens all the time. People like to smoke when clothes shopping, grocery shopping, going for a walk and even while relaxing in their home with all the windows closed. Quite frankly, it really doesn't bother me all that much.

However, when I witnessed people smoking in a hospital waiting room I almost fell over. But the real kicker was that many of the people in the hospital who were smoking turned out to be the doctors themselves—and they were on duty.

A health problem of staggering proportion, in both heart and lung disease, looms heavy on the horizon for the future medical care of these people—but the government doesn't seem the least bit fazed about this impending health debacle.

And why should it? The government derives approximately 13% of its total tax revenue from tobacco products. With approximately 350,000,000 smokers (more than the combined populations of Germany, the United Kingdom, Italy and France) they do not intend to hinder this cash cow in any way.

According to the *2007 New York Almanac* on page 486, "China is the world's largest tobacco producer; about 67 percent of the men smoke, and 4 percent of the women. About 3,000 people die each day in China from smoking, and it is estimated that smoking will kill about a third of all Chinese men under 30 today."

But if you look a little deeper you might be tempted to come up with another reason. China's population simply cannot be managed at its present numbers. All the government has done is find a way to cull the population. Again, profit is, and will remain, the bottom line—at the direct expense of its own citizens. China's history unabashedly bears this sad fact out.

However, if this is not true, then why hasn't the government—with its unlimited power—simply made it against the law to smoke in public places, especially hospitals? This would make for a very healthy beginning.

The smoking population presents an enormous problem on an already strained, inadequate healthcare system. I have no idea how they are going to handle this medical time-bomb when it finally starts to go off.

Yet, herein lies one of the main reasons why the government chose to finally renege on its promise of free medical care for all. It sees this medical tragedy coming—but purposely has chosen to do nothing about it.

Instead, it continues to rake in massive tax money from the thousands of tobacco companies scattered around the country. It simply cannot afford to cut off this huge source of easily obtainable cash.

So, in essence, the government lets the people smoke, reaps the tax revenues and then leaves the smokers to fend for themselves. If they have the means to go to a hospital they are taken care of. If they do not have the money, then they don't go.

These people—hundreds of millions—then die years before their "natural" life expectancy, the healthcare industry is not out a dime and the population is effectively culled—a win-win situation—for the CCP.

Healthcare Insurance

Insurance companies are drooling at the prospects of selling medical coverage to the Chinese people. After all, insurance companies are the richest business entities in the world—even more so than the much vaunted banking industry. And why shouldn't they be? In actuality, they sell nothing but paper accentuated by fear. And fear is the paramount ally to insurance companies the world over.

When the Chinese people wake up they are going to be outraged at the way they have been sold down the river by the very public servants that are suppose to look after them.

No more can Chinese people simply walk into a hospital and receive free medical and dental care. China is going the way of healthcare administration—and international insurance companies are climbing over each other in anticipation of the profits this nation has the potential of generating for them.

They are already in on the frenzy and the "common masses" will either have to pony up the money or go without proper medical care.

Never has such a lucrative market been so ready to be had by insurance brokers with international conglomerates ready to agree to any type of contractual arrangement just to get in on the action.

The High Price of Illness in China

In an article entitled, "The high price of illness in China," by Louisa Lim, writing for the BBC News, in Beijing, she quotes an aging village doctor as saying, "In Chairman Mao's time, you could see a doctor whether you had money or not.... Nowadays only those with money can get injections."

She further states that, "Today the old system providing near-universal access to basic healthcare has been dismantled, as the government tries to spread the cost of providing healthcare to more than one billion people."

In the article she points out that, "A World Health Organization survey measuring the equality of medical treatment placed China 187th out of 191 countries."

She also reports that the WHO's Hana Brixi said, "Healthcare providers need to raise revenues. They are not covered even for the delivery of public services.

"So they necessarily concentrate on those who have resources to spend. They provide excessive services to those who can pay, and limited services or no services at all to those who are unable to pay."

According to Ms. Lim, "The evidence suggests the poor are failing to seek medical treatment because of the cost, while the rich are paying more and more.

"Government figures show hospital visits actually dropped almost 5% between 2000 and 2003, yet hospital profits increased 70% over the same period."

In the same article she notes that bribes are given to doctors on a regular basis. "It is not suppose to happen but it is commonplace in China."

She goes on to say that, "This case highlights many of the worst problems with China's health service. Since 1980, government spending dropped from 36% of all healthcare expenditure to 17%, while patients' out-of-pocket spending rocketed up from 20% to 59%."

Lim also made reference to doctors and their departments and how they got a percentage payment from every prescription they wrote. Apparently, the more medicine the doctors prescribed, the more personal income they were able to generate.

The article concludes with an ominous statistic and a dire prediction.

"One World Bank study found 20% of China's poor blamed healthcare costs for their financial straits.

"And the country's healthcare crisis reflects its biggest problems—fighting corruption, and bridging the ever-increasing divide between the rich and the poor, the city and the countryside.

"With anger growing among the have-nots, China's leaders may find the political cost of failing to solve the problem could be higher than they ever imagined."

No More Free Housing

The government no longer gives away free housing. They are on a maniacal bent of confiscating property where people have set themselves up, forcibly evicting them if they do not agree with the ludicrously small sums of money offered to them—if any money is offered at all—then building new, high-rise condominium developments and selling the units to people who can afford them. Where the displaced people go is anybody's guess. I have literally seen acres of land cleared in a weekend—and not a trace of any of the inhabitants after that.

If people complain they are detained. If anyone resists, they are removed either by the local police or the military.

People have been killed trying to protect their own land—but again, this information is rarely permitted to reach the domestic reading public—much less the outside world.

Land

"Under all is the Land."

The above quote is the first line in the United States Realtor's Code of Ethics. In essence, if you don't own the land—you are just renting.

The concept of land ownership is not an option in China— the government owns it all—by decree in the Chinese constitution.

When the government offers its citizens paltry sums to relocate, and the people don't wish to move, they are forcibly evicted. As city boundaries expand, more and more people are being displaced. In effect, they are being herded into homelessness because of the hyper-speed, "market oriented" economic policies that China is now recklessly embracing.

An article written by, Diamond Cheng, an Associated Press Writer, reports that, "Hundreds of riot police clashed with villagers protesting against an alleged land grab by officials in the southern Chinese province of Guangdong."

In the article an activist lawyer said that, "Scores of villagers, even elderly ones, were taken away by police after being beaten."

The lawyer went on to disclose to the Associated Press that, "Local officials in Chongyuan village illegally seized the farmers' land without approval from the provincial and central governments."

Mr. Cheng reveals that, "Such allegations are common in booming Guangdong province, one of China's biggest manufacturing centers. Officials are frequently accused of forcing farmers off land, which is later sold to developers who get rich quick building factories and other projects."

These types of news reports rarely make their way to the domestic press let alone the international forum. However, they are there and they are real.

China Announces New Property Law

According to much fanfare and government controlled media hoopla it was recently reported that, "China has unveiled a landmark law that will boost the protection of private property rights."

It was touted as the, "First piece of legislation in the communist country to cover an individual's right to own assets."

But in reality this law is not, by any means, going to change the way land is appropriated in China.

As long as the government wants land, it will take it one way or another.

This law was made up simply to lull the international community into believing that communist China is moving toward a more open, democratic and *capitalistic* form of government.

And it works time and again on even some of the most astute China observers. In an article by none other than Steve Forbes, past US presidential candidate and current editor-in-chief of the influential business magazine, *Forbes*, he mistakenly asserts that, "China approves property law strengthening its middle class."

First off, most Chinese farmers are not of the middle class. They are dirt poor—pun fully intended.

Secondly, Chinese farmers know full well that this law strengthens nothing. They will have to fight for their land just as they have done for centuries.

And this is the sad fact about Western "observers" in general. They assume that once a law is enacted that it will be adhered to. Many times that doesn't even happen in the West. So what makes them so certain that it's going to come to fruition in China?

The law is pure propaganda. Nothing will change. And the farmers know it all too well—again, history as a brutal precedent.

It is painfully apparent to the masses of ordinary Chinese citizens that the old communist slogan of "Land to the tiller" no longer applies.

SOURCE:

"Fact and Comment, Right Move," *Forbes*, April 9, 2007, pg.19

CHAPTER 6

BUT THE CHINESE COMMUNIST PARTY REMAINS

Some Examples of Government Collusion, Outright Corruption and Ultimate Control

When all things are considered—family ties, nepotism, bribes, and corruption—the Chinese Communist Party can legitimately be called a "Private Party" in the strictest sense of the word.

The 2004 Transparency International Corruption Perceptions Index

"The index defines corruption as the use of public office for private gain, and measures the degree to which corruption is perceived to exist among a country's public officials and politicians.

"The Corruption Perceptions Index (CPI)] scores range from 10 (squeaky clean) to zero (highly corrupt).

"China is ranked #71, with a CPI of 3.4, along with Saudi Arabia and Syria."

SOURCE:

Transparency International, 2004. http://www.transparency.org

CHINA—THE CORRUPTION CAPITAL OF ASIA

An article on corruption in China, by Minxiu Pei, states, "Official corruption is a serious matter. For the Chinese Communist Party, it poses the most lethal threat to its survival. By all accounts, Beijing is losing the battle against graft."

The article goes on to point out that, "Hardly a day goes by without a shocking scandal coming to light in the media," further stating that, "Recently China's auditor-in-chief disclosed that an unnamed company defrauded $140 million from Chinese banks and spent nearly $40 million on bribes."

Yet, "Out of the 170,000 communist party members disciplined for wrongdoing in 2004 barely 3 percent were prosecuted. Of the corrupt officials *convicted* from 2003–2005, 52 percent received suspended sentences and served no jail time. Some even continued to draw pay." [1]

As the above article shows, bribery, fraud and corruption abound in staggering proportions. But it never seems to stop. In 2005 there were over 240,000 cases of government employee malfeasance sent to court. Those are the ones careless enough to get caught. This is just the tip of the proverbial iceberg of graft and corruption that continues to permeate China on a seemingly endless basis.

With reference to its past history, China is nothing more than an *ad hoc* state. It has very little relevance to its past, in that, there is no real constitution based on precedent or the letter of the law. Rather, law is usually determined on a case-by-case basis.

With this concept in mind, and from an ad hoc sense of historical perspective, it is no surprise to see why corruption is a major part of everyday life in China. One could conceivably make a very strong case that China is, in reality, the Corruption Capital of Asia—if not the world.

SOURCE:

[1] Pei, Minxin "The Tide of Corruption Threatening China's Prosperity," *Financial Times*, Wednesday, September 27, 2006, pg. 15

China Cracks Down on Corruption

According to the state news agency Xinhua, "A total of 67,505 government officials have been punished in China for corruption since the beginning of 2003—with 17,505 of those in the first eight months of 2006.

"The government is trying to crack down on rampant corruption, fearing it could weaken the communist party's rule."

China's chief prosecutor, Jia Chunwang, told a conference on corruption being held in Beijing that, "Corruption, if not controlled, would undermine democracy and the rule of law and engender an increase in organized crime and terrorism."

It is interesting to note that Chinese officials continually use the comforting word "democracy" then buttress it with the claim that they are trying to fight organized crime—and *terrorism*.

Of late, this has been one of the premier propaganda tactics to link any kind of action that is detrimental to the status quo of the ruling Chinese Communist Party to terrorism. It is a catch-all phrase that the Chinese government is getting a lot of mileage out of, ever since the world declaration of war on terrorism—a war that is welcomed with open arms by the vociferous proponents of worldwide Globalization. This constant fear of terrorism is one of the greatest excuses for controlling human beings ever devised by man.

So, in a masterstroke of paranoid propaganda, the Chinese government bans all dissent, under the guise of trying to stop "organized crime and terrorism" ironically in the defense of democracy.

No Explicit Rule of Law—Hidden Transparency

Even though the traditional pillars of communism—free education, free health and dental care along with free housing have been summarily eliminated, the overt communist oppression of the people by the government still exists.

As long as there is not a set rule of law, everyone is continually on edge, not knowing what to expect next. It is one of the most efficient ways to control people that I have ever witnessed in my entire life, and if nothing else, the CCP is supremely adept at controlling the "masses."

The people know full well that they have been duped but can do nothing about it—for the time being.

The communist mentality of control is still in full force. What has changed is the fact that none of the traditional benefits of the old societal contract remain.

All that's left is the boot heel of unyielding tyrannical control by the Chinese Communist Party.

Best Building Construction in China

Government buildings are the easiest to pick out when driving through any city, town or village. They are the ones surrounded by imposing fences, security guards stationed at all entrances, gleaming structures of the highest quality, manicured landscaped grounds and parking lots filled with highly polished, black limousines, with Mercedes-Benz automobiles interspersed among Lincoln Town Cars being the most favored vehicles by the communist party elite.

The Official Tourist Trap: Drive-By Diplomats and Dignitaries; Beijing, Shanghai, Hong Kong and Macao

Hong Kong is not China. Shanghai is not China. Nor is Beijing or Macao. They are only a small part of the overall picture.

These Economic Zones are not the real China. They are the economic engines fueling China's "phenomenal" growth, as the mass media love to portray it—and as the rest of the world blindly sees it.

Yet one billion people are being left completely out of the equation. And *that* is what terrifies the present status quo—thus their unrelenting headlock on power becoming increasingly more entrenched, more determined, more draconian.

So the Chinese government has decided to baffle the "experts" with trumped up statistics. Like sausages being pumped out by the thousands, wide-eyed Drive-by Diplomats and visiting foreign dignitaries are led around from meeting to useless meeting, treated to exquisite luncheons, highly orchestrated conferences, a tour of Shanghai, shopping for souvenirs in Hong Kong, a night of gambling in Macao, a daytime excursion to the Great Wall and the Forbidden City—then whisked back to the airport and sent home.

That is the way the Chinese government keeps up its false front to the rest of the world. Most "officials" *never* get out to the countryside and see the real China as it is today.

Instead, they willingly allow themselves to be decadently pampered, treated like royalty and completely bamboozled as to what is actually taking place right under their collective noses.

It would be better if they didn't come at all, because when they return to their home country they are brimming with communist propaganda, raving about the progress now underway in the "New" China. They spout on about how the socialist system is evolving into a purely unique form of "Chinese democracy."

It is a shameful occurrence that goes on with the precision of a military parade. But the most depressing thing to see is how these gullible sycophants become proponents of one of the most repressive governmental regimes in the world. These "officials" don't even have a clue as to the magnitude of pain and suffering that goes on in China—but pretend to know the whole story inside out.

Simply put, they could care less about the faceless hundreds of millions of chronically poor Chinese. What they are really concerned about are their own careers, the perks that are associated with "official overseas travel," along with keeping intact their all-important package of bloated retirement benefits.

They never go into the sweatshops and see for themselves the deplorable circumstances the workers are forced to accept, or else be immediately terminated. To these myopic visitors, sweat shops do not exist—because the Chinese government said they don't. It is a sad spectacle to witness, especially when undertaken by so-called "educated and well-informed" individuals.

Few actually go out to the countryside and smell the open sewers that are the rule, not the exception. Even fewer have any knowledge whatsoever as to the crushing poverty, human trafficking, rampant drug trade, homelessness and national depression that infects China like an out of control terminal disease.

To these Drive-by Diplomats and foreign dignitaries the only thing they are concerned about is seeing the sights, submitting a glowing report as to the state of things in China, then on to the next overseas destination for more eating, drinking, carousing and merry-making, all at company—or worse yet—taxpayer expense.

Shanghai—Economic Zone to End All Economic Zones

Shanghai is the centerpiece of China's economic and infrastructure framework—and the biggest selling point of the "New" China. From its modern, state of the art, maglev trains, to its slick shopping centers to its ultra stylish boutiques and eye-popping high-rise skyscrapers it startles the uninitiated from the very first moment they set foot in this most captivating city. And why not? Shanghai reportedly has over 4,000 skyscrapers. That is approximately twice the number of tall buildings on Manhattan—and hundreds more are on the drawing board.

"This surely must be the most advanced city in the world," thinks the newcomer. It takes everybody in, as well it should. The Chinese government has put all its marbles into this national jewel—and it shows.

There is only one problem. It is Shanghai—not China. But that is precisely the point. Intentionally mislead the naïve with highly rehearsed, institutional lies and they become instant converts, devouring all of the officially authorized professional propaganda, like starry-eyed kindergartners who believe everything their teacher tells them.

Chinese history, culture and tradition is played to the hilt—and the gaw-gaw foreign visitors that flock to China look like infants in a gigantic candy store for the first time. They can't get over talking about how "marvelous" China is. And I have to admit, I felt the same way, for the first couple of weeks. But once you live—and *work*—in China, the thin veneer of governmental falsehoods soon dissolves into a very dull finish.

Accommodations, such as the Shàngri-La Hotel in Beijing, the Shanghai Hilton, along with countless other such western type hotels are hypnotic in their elegant grace and impeccable service.

But beyond their doors, on the outskirts of town, the landscape quickly turns from opulent luxury to teeming poverty to downright squalor. But this part of China is seldom ever allowed to reveal itself to these visitors—for it is were, and word got out as to what was really going on in the "New" China—the whole world would recoil in outright horror.

The Grey Area Between State-Owned Companies and the Government

According to an article by Francesco Guerrera, "More than 2,000 of China's worst-performing state companies have won a stay of execution by being excluded from the country's new bankruptcy law until the end of 2008.

"The move, aimed at cushioning the social impact on employees of financially strained state companies will slow the disposal of bad loans held by state banks and distressed debt companies and perhaps also reduce buyout opportunities for foreigners.

"At this writing there are about 22 Chinese mega-corporations in the World's Top 500 Company Group. Most are state owned, poorly managed, and have very low efficiency ratings. Many have a very difficult time revealing what is really on the books and are constantly trying to side-step the 'transparency issue.' For this reason many Chinese companies quarterly reports are taken with a grain of salt by business people in the know.

"All Chinese banks are state owned and run by state employees that are in financial straits and disburse intentionally misleading statistics on a regular basis. It is approximated that up to 74% of Chinese banks are insolvent."

SOURCE:

Guerrera, Francesco "Struggling China State Companies Win Stay of Execution," *Financial Times*, September 25, 2006, pg. 3

The Exportation of International Corruption

In an article by Hugh Williamson, that appeared in the *Financial Times*, "According to Transparency International, the anti-corruption watchdog, Chinese state-backed companies in Africa appear to have paid bribes to secure certain lucrative business contracts."

This article went on to explain that Chinese government officials tried to defend their bribery practices as just following customary business procedures and not wanting to "interfere with the internal affairs" of other countries—a claim that government officials privately invoke all the time when doing business both inside and outside China.

Fraud and corruption is epidemic, no—pandemic—in China. It is woven into the very fabric of society. And it continues unabated.

SOURCE:

Williamson, Hugh "West Failing to Curb Bribery Overseas," *Financial Times*, September 26, 2006, pg. 5

Broken China

Thankfully, I am not the only one who sees the crime and apparently insurmountable corruption that pervades every aspect of Chinese society.

In an article for *Forbes Magazine*, James Grant wrote, "Out of a population of 1.3 billion, there must be one honest Chinese citizen. It defies belief that there wouldn't be. Yet this singular uncorrupted individual is making himself scarce. Scandal chases scandal in the People's Republic. Misdeeds seem especially prevalent in the bustling city of Shanghai, where a dustup surrounding the alleged misappropriation of assets from the $1 billion city pension fund has led to the forced resignation of three senior executives at the Shanghai Electric Group. And the Shanghai branch of Huaxia Bank has been exposed by a government audit in a scheme to underreport its nonperforming loans, according to Chinese news reports.

"But the Chinese press, though sometimes damning, is sweetness and light compared with Chinese prospectuses. Tales of bribery and embezzlement fill the "risk factors" section of the offering documents of the big Chinese banks. You'd swear you were reading the Shanghai police blotter. Insofar as the world depends on China's growth, the state of the Chinese banking system is the world's problem."

SOURCE:

Grant, James "Broken China," *Forbes*, October 2, 2006, pg.108

CHAPTER 7

BUSINESS AS UNUSUAL

Chinese Business Protocol

Bribery and corruption in China is truly "Business as Unusual."

Chinese people are not bad, per se. It is the social structure that makes them appear so.

With this in mind is bears remembering that Chinese constantly make the common error of mistaking kindness for weakness, thus their tendency to negotiate in groups, drive an extremely hard bargain, lie when appropriate, cheat when it is advantageous to do so, while all the time pretending to have only your best interests at heart.

Chinese businessmen are perversely economical with the truth. In every instance they will lie to save *Face*, get a better agreement, or break a contract all together, if it is to their benefit to do so.

Every prospective businessperson must bear this harsh observation in mind. If you get sucked into the Chinese web of "polite deception" you will lose big time. Every businessperson that has had any official transactions with the People's Republic of China will wholeheartedly attest to this fact—but only in the strictest of confidence.

In short, *honest* transparency is one of the most difficult commodities to come by in China.

The Chinese Smile

When Chinese people smile at you they are not trying to be your friend. They are trying to pave the way for a good working relationship.

But once the profit is gone, the working relationship is over. And so is the so-called friendship.

Do not be misled by Chinese people who are "so nice" and "so polite." This is simply their way of gaining favor. There are no real, long-term commitments in China, only ad hoc business associations.

A Good Business Relationship—The Chinese Bribe (Guang Shi)

This is the foundation upon which all business is conducted in China. Without it, business does not take place.

Chinese businesspersons do not consider a bribe the same way businesspeople do in the West. It is in no sense a bribe to the Chinese. It is referred to as a "business consideration"—and can come in many packages. I have seen it represented in the form of coveted sports seats, free tickets to the theater, extra curricular expenses, pre-paid dinners at the most swank restaurants—and the time honored practice of securing an exquisitely voluptuous young girl for the evening "to do with as you please."

What Contract?

As previously noted, Chinese are notorious for ignoring contractual stipulations, when the contract runs counter to their preconceived profit motives. It is something that happens with disconcerting regularity.

This type of conduct is not an aberration in any sense of the word. It happens all the time. They do it to each other every day of the year. And in turn have no compunctions dealing in this manner when conducting international business as well.

With the rash of corrupt educational establishments popping up all over China, contracts are broken at a mind-numbing rate. Schools fold overnight, leaving both students and teachers stranded with little or no recourse to getting reimbursed for school tuition or teaching salaries yet to be paid. This has become so perverse that none other than Hu Jintao personally targeted the practice of bogus international universities in his 11th Plenary statement to the Chinese people.

Day-laborers are left uncompensated after their work is completed all the time. Companies simply "forget"—or promise to pay them "at the end of the year." Every day-laborer has his or her story about being stiffed by unscrupulous employers at one time or another. It is common practice and not much can be done about it.

The most recent, and embarrassing, example was when many migrant workers, who helped to dig the new Beijing Subway for the upcoming 2008 Olympics, were not paid for the work they performed. Once news got out, they finally received some sort of compensation—only because the whole project was under scrutiny of the International Olympic Committee (IOC) which was not about to condone this type of treatment hiding behind the protection of their organization. But the fact of the matter is, the construction company involved actually tried to get away without paying them for the work they had done—a policy Chinese companies routinely employ to pocket even more ill-gotten gains.

The practice of refusing to pay migrant workers is a time honored tradition in the "New" China—with the full consent and approval of the government as a, not so subtle, way of constantly reminding the "masses" that the Chinese Communist Party is the one really in charge of the People's Republic of China.

The International Globalization Profit Margin—by the Numbers

The average Chinese worker's monthly salary, as estimated by the government, is approximately 1,500 Yuan. At 8 Yuan per dollar that comes to US $187.50.

But this is only half the story of the "average monthly income" farce purported as fact by the present status quo. Where the real crux of the matter lies is in how much the local "manual laborer" gets.

Although I could find no "government statistics" dealing with this "strata of humanity," I learned, through Chinese friends helping me to interpret while talking directly to migrant workers in the field, that they receive, on average, between 400–600 Yuan per month, if they are paid at all.

At 8 Yuan per dollar, 600 Yuan comes to roughly US $75.00 per month.

They work an average of 10 hours a day, 25 days a month.

So, US $75.00 divided by 250 hours a month (25 days x 10 hours per day) comes to a grand total of 30 US cents—*per hour.*

As simple as this arithmetic is, I actually had to do the math twice, on a calculator, before I could believe my own eyes.

So now a truer picture of China becoming a permanent member of the World Bank and the IMF, a permanent member of the WTO and a three-year member of the United Nations Human Rights Commission comes into perfect economic focus.

It makes no sense whatsoever from a humanitarian standpoint, but makes total *cents* when viewed from a financial point of reference, to treat Chinese workers in such a disdainful manner.

In the most blunt of realities, China is nothing more than an international whorehouse manufacturing cheap goods for the rest of the world in the name of Globalization.

But, here again, China is not entirely to blame.

From the Opium Wars when the Chinese Qing Dynasty sold out Hong Kong to the British for a bribe, all the way to the Tiananmen Square Massacre, when government leaders sympathizing with the "radical" pro-democracy students eventually betrayed them at the last minute, the present Chinese Communist Dynasty has, once again, sold out its hundreds of millions of migrant workers to the highest bidders of the international corporate structure—under the euphemistic guise of Globalization.

But the Chinese Communist Party does not plan to share the wealth. It simply intends to pocket the proceeds, like all other previous dynasties have done before them, bide their time and ride the gravy train as long as it lasts.

Blood and Sweat Factory—(Xue Han Gong Chang)

The companies that are most likely to be attached with this disreputable connotation usually come from Hong Kong, Taiwan, Japan and various Chinese private companies doing business on the Chinese mainland.

These companies are notorious for paying minimal wages, then working the migrant class six or even seven days a week, 10 to 15 hours a day. They give the workers minimum shelter, pay little or no workman's compensation and almost never pay any kind of medical insurance whatsoever.

Their profit is derived from how much they can squeeze out of the workers—thus the Chinese designation as a "Blood and Sweat Factory."

The company owners make money not on the profit margin of the product—but on their own workers—by making them work at full-tilt all the time or summarily firing them and hiring the next person waiting in line.

This is what is secretly referred to as "employee induced profit" and is an extremely lucrative way of doing business.

The People's Republic of China, with the benign consent of the rest of the international business community, operating under the guise of Globalization, is rapidly becoming the 21st Century's sweatshop of the world.

Sexual Harassment—a Matter of Policy

Needless to say, with this type of hierarchy firmly entrenched, sexual harassment on the factory floor is a way of life. Girls are routinely fondled, caressed and raped on a regular basis. And why not? Nobody in the international community really cares about some non-descript worker who can be replaced in a nanosecond. Nor should they be. It would hurt the bottom line. Give lip service, yes. Give a damn? Hell no.

So the rapes are endured—and remembered.

And if any woman should actually have the courage to complain she would be immediately fired and never given a letter of recommendation when looking someplace else for employment.

Sexual harassment on the job is a bombshell of a media story that will surface once more transparency is enacted in China. But for the time being this is a long way off.

One such incident occurred in the provincial capital city of Fuzhou where a group of communist politicians were having a drinking party in a downtown hotel. A maid was abducted from the staff, raped repeatedly, then murdered by throwing her out of a ninth story window.

Her body was recovered by family members and taken back to her house. Apparently, the military came and took her body away and burned it to destroy the evidence. But the family had taken the girls clothes—with the culprits' semen still in the fabric—and saved it as proof of the crime. An investigation is still pending.

Ironically, this story never hit the newspapers nor does the family hold out much hope that justice will ever be served.

The Chinese Letter of Recommendation

A letter of recommendation, with the appropriate sign and red seal attached, is the so-called holy grail of employment mobility. It is an extremely controlling factor that is held over every employee's head by their respective employers, like a guillotine inches away from the release latch. In China, if you don't have a letter of recommendation you are simply out of luck. An interview is not even considered.

I have heard more than one lurid story about employers who use this device to get many extra concessions from their employees, from unpaid overtime and outright bribes to sexual harassment and rumor induced blackmail if the employee doesn't acquiesce to the demands of the employer.

Though subtle in practice, this method of employee control runs rampant throughout China.

Insurance Company Bonanza

As noted earlier, but worth reiterating, insurance will be one of the most lucrative business endeavors in the "New" China. Sooner or later the Chinese people are going to be inundated with insurance schemes of all kinds.

This is already starting to happen. China Life Insurance Company, stock symbol LFC (and listed on the New York Stock Exchange), has a chart pointing up 120% in value from September 2005 to September 2006 alone.

Next to enter the foray are mega-corporate American insurance companies, one such establishment being the American Insurance Group, stock symbol AIG, desperate to get in on the action—with other companies following close behind.

The National Credit Card Mania Scam

"You buy more, you get more," was the headline advertisement going around our university in English. So I picked up one of the fliers and discovered it was a credit card ad directly targeting Chinese college students, who were frantically grabbing the fliers and looking at all the things they could buy—*without* money.

When you take the concept of *Face* into account, China is a salesperson's dream come true. Imagine selling cosmetics, cars, jewelry, all lines of insurance and countless other items just by saying, "Well, Mr. Wong, your neighbor just bought this type of insurance policy and his family is provided for. Don't you want to do the same thing for your family?"

Or how about, "Well, Miss Chang, your friend just bought this lovely Cartier watch with her credit card. Don't you feel you can afford it, too?"

Chinese *Face* is going to be the *silent ally* of every salesperson in China. And with the introduction of the credit card the country is going to go completely berserk spending their accrued savings faster than any other country on earth.

Safety—Not an Issue

Profit is the main goal in China—not safety. The health and welfare of its workers, and the surrounding citizenry, is of little concern to Chinese companies, nor the international conglomerates that have set up shop in the country.

In the latter part of 2005 there was an explosion at state-owned PetroChina, a company that Warren Buffet until recently held a substantial share of stocks in, where tons of benzene flowed into the Shonghua River and drifted towards the city of Harbin with its population of over four million inhabitants.

The local government tried to hide the incident but was finally forced to admit the disaster. Local government officials were fired and one actually committed suicide.

According to an article in the British newspaper, *Financial Times*, entitled "Safety worries are the flip side of success," by Geoff Dyer, in 2005, "There were 226 accidents involving chemical companies in China: a total of 321 people died and 1,521 were injured. A third of those accidents were the result of violating safety procedures."

He goes on to point out that the fines are so small that companies have little incentive to abide by safety regulations.

Again, this type of business activity is the rule, not the exception.

In a related Internet article by Sam Hopkins, dated Wednesday, September 6th, 2007, he reports that, "The news from China's Shaanxi Province is seldom bright. Every few weeks, and sometimes more frequently, I read about coal mine blasts that kill dozens there."

Further into the article he states that, "This north-central region holds 1/3 of China's coal reserves, and many of the tens of thousands of small coal mines (collieries) that operate with little or no regulation because they are privately owned.

"Recent government pledges to crack down on unsafe operations highlighted that China has over 17,000 small coal mines in operation, even following slews of Communist Party demotions and some prison sentences for renegade mine operators. The government's National Reform and Development Commission reports that deaths due to colliery accidents are down by 25.5% in the first eight months of 2006.

"But that still amounts to 2,900 dead miners so far this year!"

Win-Lose Business Approach

If a Chinese person can cheat you on a business deal he will. And it is not necessarily because he is dishonest. It is because most Chinese people approach a business transaction from an "I win/ you lose" perspective.

When there is negotiation it is not done in a manner in which to cultivate future business dealings. It is now or never. A one shot deal. And that is how it's handled.

It will take decades to convince Chinese people to try to work from a Win-Win aspect because if you win—according to the Chinese way of thinking—then the other person *must* lose. When you win, you gain *Face,* and when you lose, you lose *Face.* It's that simple.

Some True-Life Examples of the Tremendous Profits to be Made Through the Exploitation of Chinese Workers

Apple Computer

An article by AP Business Writer, Elaine Kurtenbach, showed that "Workers were exceeding the company's limits on hours and days to be worked per week."

She went on to state that, "The probe by the Cupertino, California-based company was in response to a recent report by a British newspaper, the Mail on Sunday, alleging that workers at the factory were paid as little as $50 a month and forced to work 15-hour shifts making the devices."

Ms. Kurtenbach pointed out that the company conducted its own investigation and found that, "workers assembling iPods were paid at least the minimum wage, with more than half earning more than minimum wage, excluding bonuses.

"Minimum wage for Shenzhen in southern China, where the factory is thought to be located, is about 800 yuan ($100) a month."

Do the math and you will see what the hourly wage comes to.

Autodesk

Autodesk has made tremendous profits in China over the last two years.

BASF

This European behemoth drug maker, a true transnational with over 150 years business experience, has recently announced that it is going to make its biggest investment in China in the history of the company.

The implications of this are enormous—when considering the fact that the Chinese government has reneged on it promise of free healthcare for the people. Now everyone has to pay—and BASF is setting itself up to reap *billions* of dollars in the process.

Berkshire Hathaway

Warren Buffet is reported to have had 3 billion dollars invested in state controlled PetroChina. With just the annual dividend rate of 3.10% he could afford to look the other way when it came to the wanton disregard for human rights in China.

Again, do the math. The amount of gain is just incredible—and this is only the dividend.

Blackstone Group

An article in USA Today, May 22, 2007, page 4B, *Bloomberg News*, entitled, "Blackstone sets $7.8 billion goal from stock sale, foreign stake 'Chinese connection' a selling point," the Blackstone Group has agreed "to sell a $3 billion stake to China's state-owned investment company."

The article further points out that, "Blackstone's owners, which also include insurer American International Group and 57 senior managing directors will get as much as $4.5 billion."

Divide $4.5 billion by the number of directors (57) and see what you come up with.

With such exorbitant profits to be made it becomes easier and easier to say to hell with the average Chinese worker, quietly pocket the money and whistle all the way to the bank.

Diebold

It is projected that in 10 years Diebold, the US ATM and financial services provider, could expect its business in China to account for half the company's sales.

SOURCE:

Yeh, Andrew "Diebold eyes local targets to boost its china profile," *Financial Times*, September 19, 2006, pg.21

Ford

The company plans to purchase more auto parts that are manufactured in China. The amount of money spent on this project reportedly runs into the billions.

Forward Industries

Forward Industries is also up and profits continue to soar.

General Electric

GE is on line to buy products from China that run into the billions of dollars.

Microsoft

Warren Buffet's long-time friend, Bill Gates, is also making millions in China, while pretending not to be aware of what is really going on with regard to massive human rights abuses.

Microsoft has stated that it intends to invest over $600 million in China over the next few years.

The idea of the world's two richest Americans gleefully profiting from the blood money they are extracting out of Chinese workers is shameful to say the least—all the more repulsive when we constantly hear how both men are so concerned about the poor around the world that they give billions to their favorite charities every year—accruing massive tax write-offs in the process.

Apparently their concept of human rights does not extend to the Chinese Coolie of the PRC.

Motorola

The company is reported to have invested over $40 billion in China.

Wal-Mart

According to the most recent tally Wal-Mart has 61 stores in more than 30 cities throughout China with over 29,000 employees, with more on the drawing board for years to come. It is estimated that Wal-Mart sells approximately $11 billion of Chinese made goods every year.

McDonald's

It is projected that McDonald's anticipates having 15 to 20 *thousand* outlets in China within the next five years.

Mutual Funds Soaring

According to an article in the *Investor's Business Daily*, "All but one of the top 10 performing mutual funds in 2006 focused on Chinese stocks. China region funds surged an average of 61.51% last year through December 28, according to Lipper."

How many readers of this book wouldn't be tempted to take their cut and pretend not to see what's going on?

SOURCE:

Ho, Trang "Managers See Green Star Over China, GDP of Most Populous Country Set for 5th Year of Double-Digit Gains," *Investor's Business Daily*, Wednesday, January 3, 2007, pg. A7

Introducing "Mr. China"—Robert Hsu

"IGNORE CHINA: LOSE MONEY. Read this, or you'll kick yourself for the next decade!"

These are actual headlines from a promotional brochure produced by multimillionaire China investor extraordinaire, "Mr. China" himself, Robert Hsu.

Inside the pamphlet, he states on page 2 that, "China's 1.3 billion people are willing, cheap *hands*, ready to weave and shovel, mold and weld. These hands have already turned the industrial world *upside down*." (All italics are Mr. Hsu's)

Everything he says is absolutely true. But he says not a word of the backbreaking work that these *"hands"* are forced to do at virtually slave labor wages.

So who are the ones making all the bucks? Sadly, it is the mega-corporations and the Chinese "big dogs" that are pocketing the lion's share of the money being generated by these *"hands."* The people are simply held in bondage, forced to scrounge for basic survival.

Is this wrong? Legally, no. Ethically and morally? You will have to judge for yourself.

But just as African slave labor *legally* built an economic powerhouse in the American South when "Cotton was King," the *"hands"* of labor in China are being forced to work in much the same manner.

Does the WTO and the IMF know this? Of course they do. They are part of the international consortium that is taking full advantage of the situation through their quasi-legal partnership with international corporations around the world.

The UN is also in on the take and so is the World Bank, both organizations having been immersed in numerous scandals in the past with some of these unscrupulous situations still unresolved.

In years past, UN Peace Keepers have been accused of rape and torture, the former UN Secretary General, Kofi Anon's son implicated in a money scandal, and now at the very time of this writing, no less than the president of the World Bank himself, Mr. Paul Wolfowitz, is being accused of showing favoritism in arranging both job promotions and a generous pay package for his *girlfriend*.

These are the very organizations that are overseeing the massive exploitation of the general Chinese populace. Does the age-old saying of "the fox guarding the henhouse" come to mind?

With regard to taking notice as to what is happening, most people simply choose to look the other way—just as Mr. Robert Hsu is doing.

Please don't get the wrong idea. I am not against *responsible* capitalism. And I am not one of the liberal left yelling from the rooftops for the destruction of the capitalistic system. Not by a long shot.

I am simply stating fact—nothing more, nothing less.

But I doubt that the people making the money off these *"hands"* even care what the actual situation is. The allure of mega-riches can turn even the most pious into a glutton for more profits, more money, more power, more riches, more, more, more....

Such is human nature. And I have heard the flaccid excuse—"If I don't do it somebody else will"—so many times, that I am actually beginning to wonder if anybody really *does* care.

My purpose in taking this tact is to merely put the truth out on the table for all to see. If the truth is out there, and if people still persist in taking part in the economic rape of China, then they must be ready to pay the piper when the time comes. And, unless I am grossly mistaken, the time is rapidly approaching when drastic change will again take place.

The word "revolution" is again slowly creeping into conversations throughout China. It may be closer than anybody even anticipates.

Yet Robert Hsu continues his sales pitch by noting that, "China is full of cowboys. They may not wear Stetsons, but they wear Rolex watches and sport a winning smile. Just a few years ago, they were communist party cadre, determined to battle foreign capitalists.

"But Deng Xiaoping woke them up in 1978 with a stunning promise: If you have a business idea, the State will back you.

"Overnight, local communes built clothing factories, broom factories, belt factories, beer factories. Some of the farmers worked the machinery, some bought supplies, some toured the countryside as a sales force.

"But the clothing was shoddy, the brooms fell apart, the beer bottles were unwashed and the sales force developed a reputation as sexual adventurers. Billions of yuan simply vanished into the managers' pockets.

"And the successful cowboys became Robber Barons. Today, they run the "State-Owned Enterprises (SOEs) that most Western mutual fund managers invest in. That these SOEs are riddled with corruption is openly acknowledged."

I admire Mr. Tsu for unabashedly admitting what diplomats and dignitaries refuse to fess up to in public. At least he has the courage to say the obvious.

He further sticks his neck out by giving a concrete example. "Bank of America pays $3 billion for a 9% stake in a troubled China Construction Bank, knowing full well that their new best friend's books look like Swiss cheese and smell worse. But what Bank of America gets in return is access to 14,000 retail outlets.

"Some would argue that the potential is so great, Bank of America can afford to hold its nose"

Mr. Tsu then further implores his potential subscribers by saying, "If you read nothing else I send you, please read *The Biggest Scandal in Investing History*. It blows the lid off the cozy and corrupt system that extends from Wall Street fund managers to Shanghai and Hong Kong back streets. It's a tale of greedy brokers that rob their own clients, even while the State-Owned Enterprises they push go south.

"I expose the most *corrupt* SOEs and show you which exchanges are guilty of lying, manipulation, insider trading—and outright stealing. And I tell you which big, famous funds are implicated in this scandal. This is your complete handbook on how NOT to invest in China."

All this was taken verbatim from one of his mail-outs to prospective clients. It was one of the most honest appeals—and full testimony— to what is actually taking place in the "New" China of today—but no one seems to be paying much attention as to how the money is actually made.

They are too busy looting the populace to care about anything else.

The consummate salesman, Mr. Tsu pushes on by saying, "Imagine you had just arrived in China and I were to show you around. I could awe you with the Three Gorges Dam or terrify you with rush hour in Beijing. I could spout enough statistics—a brand-new city the size of Philadelphia is founded every 30 days, and so on—to make your jaw drop…and your eyes glaze over."

He then confesses that, "I was born in Taiwan and know China like the back of my hand. I was educated in California and have made my own personal fortune in stocks—many of them China stocks. I was a global hedge-fund manager at Goldman Sachs, and now I am helping my American friends earn *their* fortune in China."

This very astute entrepreneur then employs the kicker in his spiel by saying, "In joining me today, you have put yourself in a remarkable and quite elite group. Most investors depend on mutual funds to give them a little exposure to this China Miracle. But rarely do Western mutual fund managers stray out of their shiny hotels when visiting China.

"*Very few* of them speak Mandarin or Cantonese.

"And almost *none* of them would understand when they were being lied to.

"And if you think a New York cabby can spin a tall tale, you should just *hear* a Chinese oil executive go to town on a Western mutual fund manager!"

The reason I have quoted Mr. Tsu so extensively is not to plug his investment acumen—which is extensive. Rather, it is to show you that what I have been saying about China is not some made up diatribe.

Mr. Tsu was born in Taiwan. He *knows* what is going on.

My hat is off, with a word of thanks, to Mr. Robert Tsu, for his unadulterated honesty.

Chinese Crime Really Does Pay—Beijing Bulletin

"BEIJING (AFP)—A home appliance retail tycoon caught up in a high profile bank fraud case is now China's richest person, Forbes magazine said in an annual ranking that shows personal wealth in China skyrocketing as its economy booms.

"Topping the list with a net worth of 2.3 billion dollars was Huang Guangyu, the 37-year-old founder of Gome Appliances, China's largest electrical appliance chain.

"Huang's fortune nearly doubled over the past year as newly affluent Chinese consumers snapped up Gome's refrigerators and other products, Forbes said in its 2006 ranking of China's rich.

"Chinese media have reported that Huang is under investigation over 165 million dollars in loans extended by the Bank of China between 1997 and 2004.

"The probe reportedly centers on his older brother, real estate developer Huang Junqin. Gome has denied the reports.

"Huang's swelling fortune is emblematic of China's new super-rich set who are amassing unprecedented wealth at a rapid clip and at younger ages than ever, the magazine said.

"The combined wealth of China's 400 richest people jumped 51 percent to 110 billion dollars since Forbes' list last year."

SOURCE:

http://news.aunz.yimg.com/xp/fafp/20061103/03/3389821016.jpg"

The Millions Left Behind

In an article entitled, "China's rural millions left behind," by Rupert Wingfield-Hayes, BBC News, Beijing, he acknowledges that, "In China, if they can, people try not to think about the countryside at all.

"When they do, it is not of a rural idyll, but a grim, dirty place where people are poor and life is harsh."

Mr. Wingfield-Hayes goes on to point out a persistent hidden social malaise wherein he reports that, "China's urban population has a strong tendency to look down on country folk. The word for 'farmer' in Chinese has a distinctly pejorative flavour."

He points out that, "Rural people are of a very low quality" is a phrase you often hear in Beijing.

"And rural people are not just treated like second class citizens, they are.

"Almost everything in the countryside is worse than in the cities, according to popular belief.

"People say the schools are bad, the teachers awful; there are very few doctors, and hardly any clinics or hospitals; local communist party officials are invariably corrupt, and often abuse their power for personal gain."

The Worst Scenario for America—and the World

The absolute worst thing that could happen would be for China to become democratic and free-enterprising at the same time. This would put America and world markets at an extreme disadvantage simply because of the massive population that China has going for it. There would be no way that the USA, let alone other Western countries, could compete. The number of people in China is just too overwhelming.

So now we begin to understand why America—along with other countries and organizations—are being so light on the Middle Kingdom. They want to take part in the economic bloodletting that is already taking place in China by exploiting a meek and destitute migrant workforce for record profits—money that will go into the pockets of multinational corporations along with a few mega-rich Chinese, while the status of the masses remains constant.

The last thing that America needs—or the world wants—is another Asian Tiger the size of China. The Four Tigers of Singapore, South Korea, Taiwan and Hong Kong are bad enough. Can you imagine how high the competition bar would be raised if China actually did become a democracy?

America—and most European countries—would, in essence, cease to be able to produce virtually anything in a competitive nature. Thus the real reason why America—and the rest of the world—are not screaming about human rights or any other Chinese violations for that matter.

Where human rights comes into direct conflict with corporate profit, the consideration of the corporation always wins out.

As for dealing with communists, and their avowed desire to control every aspect of Chinese life, all free democracies *willingly* divert their attention to the other side of the room.

The international community's chorused refrain—led by the United States of America—is, "Show me the money!"

THE HYPOCRISY OF THE HUMAN RIGHTS CHAMPION: BENIGN AMERICAN COMPLICITY

"In America, politics is Big Business."

J. P. MORGAN

Treasury Secretary Henry Paulson has said that he is all in favor of the market economic reforms that are going on in China. I find it disturbing, to say the least, that he is not voicing more concern about the plight of the hundreds of millions of Chinese people that are not allowed take part in the economic boom that is now underway in China. Then again, if he did, he might anger the Chinese Communist Party—and that is one thing few people have the courage to do.

The following is a verbatim quote from the *2007 New York Times Almanac* in the World History section on page 445.

"Since 1990, China has been the focal point of U.S. foreign policy and economic strategy. Despite the Chinese government's overt acts of repression and manifest evidence of serious human rights abuses, Presidents Bush and Clinton both aggressively pursued an economic alliance that has benefited both countries. Tens of billions of dollars were invested in China in the 1990s and, not surprisingly, China became the chief supplier of low-cost consumer goods and other items to the U.S. In 1997, China sent exports worth $62 billion to the U.S. but imported only $13 billion. By 2003 China's exports to the U.S. had soared to $152 billion and China held over $600 billion in U.S. treasuries (debt)."

As a matter of public record, corporate USA appears to be more concerned with profit than it is with anything else.

CHAPTER 8

SOME "EXTRA CURRICULAR" OBSERVATIONS

Chinese Museums—and the People's Relics

When touring museums and temples in China I was constantly amazed at how the artifacts, statues and national relics were in such pristine condition. I kept commenting on how the works on display looked brand new but were actually thousands of years old.

Finally, my Chinese colleague confessed that almost all the works were, in fact, replicas of the original pieces. "Replicas," I blurted out. "Then where are the originals?"

My friend assured me that to see the real objects was virtually impossible. "They are kept in safe-keeping for the people," he informed me.

Then he added that theft is so bad the government decided to stash all of China's national treasures in a secret place that nobody knows about—again, for the benefit of the people.

I asked him if he was aware of what other dynasties had done with China's national treasures and he said he wasn't sure. When I told him that they had a history of ferreting them out of the country, or selling them to international purchasers on the black market, he actually turned pale.

Then he said, "But every once in awhile they have a TV documentary where a reporter goes and does a series on national treasures and airs the show nationwide."

I asked, somewhat obliquely, who owns all the television stations. He stared at me, blinking in rapid-fire succession. "The government," he finally muttered, under his breath.

I just looked at him.

"But what about the people?" he stammered.

Please note how ubiquitous the word "people" becomes when talking about the "New" China. It is the catch-all phrase that is always trotted out when all other defense mechanisms fail.

Bear in mind, this is the *People's* Republic of China.

Secret Off-Shore Bank Accounts

All I can attest to is what I have heard—and the rumors are rampant. It was talked about, over and over again, among my friends and colleagues that the elite Chinese hierarchy, along with a myriad of other, lesser higher-ups, have stashed billions of dollars in secret overseas bank accounts.

According to an article in the Straits Times entitled, *Shades of grey in China's widening income gap*, by Sim Chi Yin, she states that, "The latest annual list of the country's richest by publishing group Hurun Report shows that about 30 percent of China's wealthiest entrepreneurs are members of the Communist Party, and 38 percent of the top 100 are members of one of two leading political bodies—the National People's Congress and the Chinese People's Political Consultative Conference."

If nothing else, the communist Chinese have learned their history well. They do not intend to get caught with everything they have pilfered from the people landlocked on the mainland. When the day comes for them to evacuate they will take national treasures and mountains of money with them.

This has been done so that when—not *if*—another revolution takes place they will be guaranteed a comfortable retirement in some undisclosed foreign location for the rest of their lives.

And remember, these are international currencies, Euros, British Pounds, United States Dollars—not Chinese Yuan. When the revolution comes—and if history is to be any guide—the next dynasty to take over will render the present Yuan currency obsolete, and therefore useless.

This is a fairly common practice when revolutions occur—especially in developing countries. This way the corrupt officials, who were the reason for the revolution in the first place, are not able to abscond with their ill-gotten gains.

However, if the currency is printed by other countries, there is very little recourse to recover the money and since it is legal tender in the international arena, corrupt Chinese Communist Party officials are, in every sense of the word, home free.

Do I have any proof of this? Of course not. That is why they are *secret* off-shore bank accounts.

At this juncture it is interesting to note where so much of this ill-gotten profit is being stashed—in gold bullion and international currencies.

Much of these mega-profits derived from Globalization lead to one city, Zürich. And for good reason. It is historically veiled in a labyrinth so steeped in secrecy, and protected by such an elaborate security system, that even the CIA can't get a real fix on who owns what.

Even though the Form B (ultra secret) Swiss bank account system has been technically abolished, that does not mean there are no more clandestine bank accounts. Contrary to accepted wisdom there are still many ways to set up, finance, and administer secret accounts, of which Chinese Communist Party officials are rumored to have an abundance of.

SOURCES

The Straits Times, *Shades of grey in China's widening income gap*, by Sim Chi Yin, Wednesday, July 18, 2007, page 1 and 2

Daily Tension—Survival at All Costs

The daily tension associated with living in China is so thick that you can cut it with a chain saw—as though everybody was walking on eggshells—afraid to make any sudden change for fear of doing something wrong and getting blamed accordingly.

From the never-ending battle with intentionally arcane bureaucratic regulations, coupled with the fraud and corruption associated with all levels of government civil servants, to the endless confrontations to establish *Face*, and then maintain it on a daily basis, Chinese people live their lives as though they are strapped into a social roller coaster from which they can never escape.

Business negotiations routinely break down into vehement shouting matches, a minor faux pas can ignite into a wide-opened imbroglio, and a simple breach of social etiquette can be mistaken as an intentional insult and, again, loss of *Face*.

On numerous occasions I was witness to outright hysterical screaming and psychologically verifiable eruptions by the director of our college, so much so that many of the secretaries would completely avoid any contact with him—taking the long way around his office or slipping into the women's rest room to avoid meeting him in the hallway.

People also have to be constantly vigilant when shopping so as not to get intentionally cheated.

Wage earners—especially migrant day workers—are acutely aware that they might not get paid for their services and have no legal recourse to get their money.

When the software college that I was associated with finally went bankrupt, after extravagant amounts of monetary mismanagement, many of the Chinese professors were summarily fired, while others were paid a lesser amount than agreed upon. If anybody complained they were denied payment altogether—and steadfastly refused the all-important letter of recommendation as alluded to earlier for future employment reference.

THE CHINESE NATURAL ENVIRONMENT— OR LACK THEREOF

Some General Environmental Observations

With regard to the Chinese environment and the incomprehensible amount of environmental pollution that is involved, volumes have already been written on the subject. Bearing that fact in mind I will touch only on some of the more perverse aspects that are witnessed on a daily basis.

In an article in the Shanghai Daily dated, Thursday 20, October 2005, Paul Wolfowitz, president of the World Bank, stated that, "Lanzhou is one of the most polluted cities in the *world*."

China is, in a very perverse way, nothing but a toxic waste dump in many parts of the country.

In 2005 alone, sulfur dioxide emissions rose, on average 15%.

In many cities trees refuse to grow.

In some sections of the country, the soil is tarnished with pollutants, riverbeds are completely dried up, mountains of discharged residue blanket the landscape. Streets are awash in raw sewage, a constant stench putrefying the air.

DIRECT PERSONAL ASSAULT ON THE ENVIRONMENT

Phlegm Forever

Chinese people spit everywhere—and that includes the women, too. They spit in hallways of shops and stores, on the sidewalks and stairs, in supermarkets, public transportation vehicles and even in hospitals. It is a national pastime that needs to be addressed on a countrywide basis.

Yet, there is an intriguing aspect to the way many Chinese people actually spit—and I say this in all sincerity. On many occasions, when I observed people dutifully expectorating, they seemed to do it with a vengeance—almost as though they were spitting on the Chinese Communist Party itself. I know this sounds far-fetched but it actually appeared that way to me.

No Diapers

Most Chinese babies wear pants—with no crotch. In other words any little tyke that has not been housebroken walks around with all his or her "privates" for the whole world to see. It is kind of cute in an innocent sort of way—until it comes time to "go."

And go they do, out in public, in the bushes, in the rives, in the open sewers—anywhere is OK. The attending parent simply holds the baby up, spreads the legs and lets everything fly. It is quite a sight to see and I am sure there is a public health problem somewhere in the mix, but nobody seems to mind one bit.

When Nature Calls

But what is even more striking is to see grown-ups doing it. I have seen taxi drivers, businessmen, women of all walks of life, take to the bushes or simply let it all hang out right on the side of the road without giving it a second thought.

When you consider this sort of activity in cities where the population could well exceed a million people you can start to get the picture of what it is like to go for a leisurely Sunday afternoon stroll in the park. Speaking of which this is the most opportune time to view this kind of social behavior first hand.

Litter

Litter is ever-present and in copious amounts. Chinese throw trash everywhere. They don't seem to consider the mess that they are contributing to, let alone the social consequences involved.

Cigarette butts cover the sidewalks, McDonald's wrappers blowing in the wind, drivers tossing litter out of their car windows, household garbage piled in the streets to rot. Much of this eventually ends up in the water system and contributes greatly to the poor quality of water throughout China.

WATER POLLUTION IN CHINA

It is estimated that nearly 90% of all drinking water in China is polluted in one way or another.

In 2005 government figures released by the Xinhua news agency found that the drinking water of almost 300 million people in China was actually considered contaminated and unsafe to drink. Keep in mind, this is the news as reported via the government controlled media. Due to the Chinese government's penchant for lying, the figure is no doubt much higher.

Non-Potable Tap Water

China is one of 16 countries in the world that is designated as not having enough potable water. Factory pollution, along with highly contaminated, untreated runoff, is commonplace.

Underground water reserves are becoming thoroughly inundated with contaminants because of seepage and a lack of governmental concern with regard to fighting pollution in general.

AIR POLLUTION, PEOPLE POLLUTION AND PUBLIC TRANSPORTATION

Air Unfit to Breathe

Breathing is a chore; asthma is rapidly becoming a national health issue.

In some cities the air is so heavy with industrial crud that people wear masks all day long. In many parts of the countryside the sky actually runs from dark grey to a ghoulish black color, with particles of soot constantly drifting down from above.

People ride their rusty bicycles through streets covered in powdered dust and are continuously brushing themselves off.

In the bleakest of examples—reminiscent of a Salvador Dali surreal-istic painting— some cities would remind the casual observer of what the aftermath of an atomic war might look like.

CO_2

According to a letter published in the *Financial Times* by Ruth Lea, Director, Center for Policy Studies, London, UK, "By 2030 China will be the largest producer of CO_2 emissions, producing approximately 7.4 billion tons between 2002 and 2030. India's projected increase between 2002 and 2030 in comparison, is 'only' 1 billion tons."

People Pollution

People on the actual streets travel by any means available, some on foot or clinging tenaciously to motor scooters spewing dirty exhaust into the already foul air, many in cars and trucks that appear to be in conditions ranging from dilapidated pushcarts held together with baling wire to sleek foreign sedans racing their way through the ever present city congestion.

Accidents are literally an everyday occurrence. Traffic signals are obeyed only in critical intersections in large cities and very loosely at that.

Pedestrians literally take their lives in their own hands when crossing the street. Cars simply don't stop for people and many a person is killed every year in China's rough and tumble traffic. People actually cross six lane highways on foot, at night, on a regular basis.

City Buses

Driving a city bus through the horrendous traffic of China is not a job—it is an *art*. Most buses in cities outside of major metropolitan areas are in true "third world" condition, filthy dirty, with continuous mechanical problems, and no apparent emission controls whatsoever.

Some buses are in such bad shape that the one my wife was riding on one day broke down at the side of the road. The driver bolted for the door and disappeared. She found out later that this was standard operating procedure for simple self-preservation. Passengers have been known to take their daily stress and bound up frustration out on the bus driver if there is a mechanical mishap. Apparently, drivers have learned to take off, hide until all the riders are gone, then come back and wait for the repair truck to arrive.

Taxis

Approximately 6,000 new cars hit the road *daily* in China, yet the infrastructure is woefully unprepared for this onslaught.

Some Chinese experts have calculated that it takes up to approximately one percent of China's total GDP related to time wasted in traffic.

Taxis are everywhere. They are usually in borderline condition, mufflers missing, windows broken and many times fumes emanating from just underneath the dashboard.

If driving a city bus in China is an art, then riding in a Chinese taxi is truly an extreme sport—for both the cabbie and the passenger alike. When you get into a taxicab—especially in the shotgun position— hold on to your seat, say your prayers and make sure you medical insurance policy is paid in full.

If you wait for a taxi, you will be waiting a long time. With human pollution such as it is in China what you must do is grab a taxi or else the person right next to you will take the one you have just hailed. It is common practice in the dog-eat-dog mentality of the "New" China.

The 2005 Environmental Sustainability Index (ESI)

"The ESI is a composite index tracking 21 indicators, including natural resources, pollution levels, and environmental management efforts, that characterize and influence environmental sustainability on a national scale.

"Out of 146 countries reported, China ranks #133, between Iran #132 and Tajikistan #134."

SOURCE:

Esty, Daniel C., Levy, Mark, Srebotnjak Tanja, and de Sherbinin, Alexander. *2005 Environmental Sustainability Index: Benchmarking National Environmental Stewardship.* New Haven: Yale Center for Environmental Law and Policy.

Fuzhou—China's Center for Human Traffic Trade

Fuzhou City, just across the strait from Taiwan, is considered the center for human traffic trade—especially young female children. Some estimates rate this line of business more profitable than illicit drugs.

Kidnapping, and the buying and selling of young children, is a thriving business—and is conducted with the benign complicity of Fuzhou

Communist Party officials. Otherwise, how could it ever exist? The amount of children traded is unavailable, and in many circles it is categorically denied, but it flourishes nonetheless.

Large numbers of these children end up being sold to foreigners under the guise of legal adoptions, many times to well-meaning, but naïve Christian organizations acting out of the miss-directed goodness of their hearts.

From time to time, there is the occasional story of whole groups of illegal Chinese immigrants being discovered, some dead, some barely alive, in cargo containers in the Seattle Washington Port Facility. You simply cannot ship containers of human beings without inside help—statistics or no statistics.

This is a huge revenue source for crooked government officials at all levels and will continue to be as long as the CCP is running the country.

Fuzhou—China's Center for Illicit Drugs

Fuzhou City is also the center for illicit drug distribution and the main traffic station for export to Western Europe. This again, is done with a casual nod from the local powers that be.

Police are allegedly involved in "taking care of" drug lords and some are even rumored to be on the Chinese underworld's direct payroll. Again, this is adamantly denied by Fuzhou authorities, and extremely hard to verify, as are most other statistics detrimental to the existence of the present status quo.

What is ironic is that people from Fuzhou, who apply for a passport or visa to travel to foreign countries, are put under additional scrutiny when submitting for these official papers—by the Fuzhou government itself.

Furthermore, when people go to different regions within China they are viewed with a jaundice eye at every juncture by authorities

113

in different provinces throughout the country, simply because their place of origin is Fujian province, of which Fuzhou is the capital city.

Child Abuse and Domestic Violence

This is another area that is very difficult to obtain reliable information on because of the social stigma involved. According to professors that I know very well, it is yet another socially explosive issue with underlying currents swirling just beneath the shallow surface.

I have been assured by more than a few people that child abuse is very much a part of the Chinese social landscape—especially child molestation and actual rape. One only needs to realize how much of a stigma rape still carries in the West. Then you can get an idea of how much it is hushed up in China. Here again, verifiable information is extremely hard to come by.

This also holds true with domestic violence. In some cases domestic violence is handled by village leaders because it tends to be of a more open or known disturbance, whereas child molestation and rape is much more discrete and rarely addressed in public proceedings.

Where the Chinese government can, and when the need arises, it manufactures its own evidence at will. Yet the people are always required to have "proof positive" of any wrongdoing when submitting any type of complaint to the authorities.

And this is where the classic communist refrain is heard the loudest: If you have no verifiable evidence—then the crime did not take place.

You must have proof.

Prostitution—It's Against the Law—But it Isn't

This is one of the most elaborately conceived forms of public exploitation of women in China. Prostitution is supposed to be against the law, but has official sanctioning in cities all over the country.

If the government sought to have prostitution eradicated, if it does not authorize it, then why is it so prevalent?

Mainly, because it is again a source of unreported revenue—in which a consortium of government, police and military officials (some of the biggest customers)—conspire to take their cut and then pretend to be ignorant of the whole situation. It is one of the biggest "open secrets" in the "New" China of today.

What could only be described as comic irony is that around many government buildings are some to the most interesting red light districts in the world. Row upon row of them.

Why are they situated so close to government buildings? For simple security. Build close to the castle (government buildings) for protection and a degree of legitimacy. If it is close to the center of power and not closed down—then it must be OK.

Flooding—Naturally

That China has flooding is a matter of record. Why they don't really control it is not as well known.

Periodic flooding kills thousands of people in China each year—sometimes millions.

China's population has always been an administrative headache—and one of the best ways to help keep it under control is to let nature take its course naturally.

There is no other reason why flooding continues to happen, year after year, while nothing is being done about it. After all, flooding is not that difficult to curtail. It is not high-tech and it does not cost all that much—labor wise—in China, to prevent.

"If you can put men into orbit, explode atomic weapons and build up a huge army but yet cannot provide for the basic needs of the people then what good is the system of government that prevails in China today?" asked a professor friend of mine over dinner one night. I didn't have the heart to tell him that the cruel reality is, the government doesn't care.

Strict Limit to Lawyers

The number of lawyers in China is firmly established by the government. The status quo does not intend to let too many lawyers into the system, thus causing more upheaval in the people's right to demand that their basic civil liberties be respected.

Also, by doing this the government can keep most complaints to a minimum, thereby appearing to the world to be a tranquil and "modern" country in "complete harmony" with its total surroundings.

By keeping a strict adherence to the actual number of attorneys that are allowed to practice, it insures that lawyers will only represent those who can pay the most money—thus effectively eliminating any private representation of the majority of people by experienced legal counsel.

Cornell Law

In an article in the distinguished FORUM, Cornell Law, Summer/ Fall 2006 edition, page 23, it was pointed out that, "The concept of a legal system goes back to the Tang Dynasty which usually dealt with administrative and criminal law—but nothing relating to the rights of common individuals, let alone the concept of human rights."

The article goes on to say that, "The judicial system, moreover, though far less dependent than it was even five years ago, is still fraught with problems such as how to produce enough lawyers, law firms, and legal knowledge.

"Additionally, 'local protection,' or the perception that one will not receive a fair legal decision in a province other than his or her own, extends beyond the courts and into many legal and economic systems throughout China. Finally, the country is now experiencing a shortage of lawyers willing to work pro bono and to work in poorer areas."

SOURCE:

FORUM, Cornell Law, Summer/Fall 2006 edition, pg.23, Cornell University Law School

Forced Abortions Activist Lawyer Detained

In an article written by Steven Ertelt in Linyi, China, LifeNews.com Editor, August 18, 2006, and obtained off the Internet, entitled, *Trial of China Forced Abortion Activist Ends in Chaos, Chen's Lawyers Arrested*, Mr. Ertelt points out that the trial of activist lawyer, Chen Guangcheng, "Ended in chaos Friday. Chen's crime was to bring to international attention, a brutal family planning campaign that involved the forced abortions or sterilizations of 10,000 women.

"Li Fangping, another attorney who was falsely arrested and prevented from helping Chen, said the activist was appointed to state lawyers who knew nothing of his case. He said the repeated denial of rights caused Chen to be physically ill.

"He was so angry that he threw up several times," Li told Reuters, quoting Chen's brother who attended the trial.

It goes on to report that, "Hundreds of police surrounded the court-house in Yinan County, Shandong province where the trial was held and prevented Chen supporters from entering, including Chen's wife Yuan Weijing. Others were placed under house arrest.

"The prevention of Chen's attorneys from helping him appears to be masterminded by leading Chinese national officials," one human rights observer told Reuters.

"There is no doubt in my mind that there is a concerted crackdown on rights lawyers under way," Nicholas Bequelin, a researcher for Human Rights Watch, said. "This seems to have been sanctioned by the highest level and they're really sending a chilling message to lawyers in China."

"Chen brought the forced abortion family planning campaign to the attention of American media outlets and said as many as 10,000 women in the province were forced to have abortions or sterilized against their will.

"Anyone who attempted to flee the brutality was apprehended, beaten, and held hostage in city prisons until their relatives came forward and paid large fines for their release."

"Chen's attorneys say the Chinese government is turning a blind eye because it often allows local governments great leeway in putting down political unrest.

"Linyi officials have persuaded some top Chinese leaders that Chen's efforts are supported by overseas groups and they successfully lobbied the Foreign Ministry and the powerful Propaganda Department to ban any discussion of Chen's case in the state media or on the Internet."

Animal Rights—A Dog's Life

In an article by Howard W. French, retrieved from the Internet, published August 10, 2006, he reported that, "Officials in Mou Ding County in southwestern Yunnan Province had ordered the mass extermination of dogs, pets as well as strays, after three people died in a rabies outbreak.

"As a crowd gathered around a large tree in the village of Xiajiashan, owners complied, one after another, with commands to string up their dogs.

"According to official figures, 54,429 dogs were killed during the Yunnan campaign. Reports in the Chinese news media say that some people out walking their dogs had the animals seized by gangs of vigilantes, who clubbed the dogs to death on the spot."

The report goes on to note that, "As remarkable as the killings themselves, however, has been the response. As word of the killings has spread here, pet owners have begun to mobilize—speaking out online and circulating petitions—to try to stop the killings. The reaction of groups and individuals, often through the Internet, also provides a striking illustration of the emergence of true public opinion in China, unmediated by the official press or censors."

One of the posted messages noted that, "This is just another stupid decision by several foolish officials taken in a small room, totally unreflective of the people's will."

Other posted comments made comparisons with China's current situation saying, "We don't have human rights, let alone dog rights," wrote a person by the name of Kui Kui Xiang Ri.

His posting stated that, "I've seen too much life abuse, let alone abuse of dogs. Anyway, it's the local emperors who have their say, and we ordinary folks are not much different from dogs in their eyes."

Mr. French further states that, "Experts say the persistence of the disease reflects the breakdown of the rural health care system, once one of the proudest achievements of Chinese Communism."

China Plans Rare Animal Hunt

In an Internet report by Reuters, August 9, 2006, from Beijing, "China plans to auction licenses to foreigners to hunt wild animals, including rare species.

"The government will auction the licenses based on the numbers in each category of animal, ranging from a starting price of $ 2,000 for a wolf, the only predator on the list, to as much as $40,000 for a yak," the Beijing Youth Daily said. "There are believed to be fewer than 10,000 mature wild yak in the world."

I have personally seen hawkers at street stalls selling live frogs hanging by their necks, puppies jammed into boxes being sold on street corners, goldfish in plastic bags filled with murky water, barrels filled with turtles crawling over each other, ducks packed into cages and yanked out by the beak when sold, and birds smothering to death in overcrowded cages.

But the most devastating of all is to visit a Chinese zoo. If the plight of these animals ever gets out, especially of the animals in outlying district zoos, animal activists throughout the world would be aghast at what is taking place.

The Great Firewall

By far, the biggest emerging fear of the government is that of the Internet—and the freedom of speech it can afford to all its citizens—thus the Great Firewall, an intricate Internet screening device that stops, or disrupts, communication between people the government considers detrimental to its survival—read *democratic activists*—or "subversives" as the government chooses to label them.

Information is power and the Chinese communist government loves both. Thus, their relentless determination to limit all information coming into, and going out of, China.

Worms, viruses and other such interesting Internet headaches are a constant occurrence. E-mail messages are routinely scanned for "key" words and not delivered if found to be even the least bit suspicious.

In recent years the government has begun to crack down even harder under the guise of "fighting terrorism" as their excuse. I find it cruelly amusing that a communist government would be so concerned about terrorism—considering the social anarchy they wantonly inflict on their own people with complete impunity.

Rampant strains of official viruses are constantly attacking private computer systems—while the government and military computer networks experience very few problems with regard to outside "hacking" of intelligence data.

Thousands of law-abiding citizens are put into jail every year, just for posting and/or reading expressions of freedom and demanding a more open, transparent and free democratic Chinese society.

As the Internet proliferates—so does the Chinese people's desire to be free.

Nationwide Crackdown on Cell Phones

The Chinese government is drafting legislation that is going to require all cell phones to be registered with the national government. The user's name, phone number and address will be on secret file.

In China, telephone calls are routinely monitored and cut off if the "line moderator" thinks that something is being discussed that shouldn't be.

George Orwell is smiling from his grave with the deepest of admiration for the current ruling Chinese Communist Dynasty.

CHAPTER 9

THE HIDDEN AGENDA: THE TAIWAN ISSUE AND THE PERFECT SAFETY VALVE—DEATH TO A DEMOCRACY

One China, Two Policies

Before any international commitment with heads of state are solidified with other countries, they must first publicly affirm their adherence to the above proclaimed concept of one China, two policies. If they do, then the People's Republic of China proceeds to talk business. If they do not, no deal.

Most all heads of foreign states have agreed with China on this principle—for the sake of profit. And virtually all "smaller countries" have no qualms about agreeing to such a philosophy to get their cut of so-called Chinese aid and investment programs now being touted around the globe.

The "Taiwan Issue"—Non-Debatable

As alluded to earlier, the centralized concept of thought control is frightfully successful in China. The paramount example is the "Taiwan Issue."

When discussing this topic, which I was expressly forbidden to do in class by administration officials, but did so anyway, I found virtually all my students in agreement that Taiwan was a part of Mainland China.

Moreover, I was told that it was America and Japan that were interfering in the internal affairs of China because they wanted to control China's shipping lanes for further military and economic exploitation.

In truth, this argument has a fair amount of validity attached to it. But the fact that *all* the students felt this way is an immediate sign of indoctrination, *not* education. In unison, the students demanded that the topic was "non-debatable" and there was no point in going any further, some physically waving me off altogether.

I admire my Chinese university students for their love and determination to defend their country at all costs. This is something that most citizens of all nations gallantly purport to do. So when I asked them if China should go to war if Taiwan actually declared independence, they all answered yes—including everyone of the females. There was not *one* student who disagreed with this stance.

Yet, when I posed the question, "If *you* were conscripted to go kill Chinese who lived in Taiwan, who wanted only to be free from communist domination, would you be willing to go fight— and *kill*—to achieve that goal?" This is where the line of mental resistance began to break down. About half of the class was very hesitant to raise their hands.

And this is precisely the reason why the communist government does not allow discussion on this, and many other, politically sensitive issues.

Discussion and debate, with logical reasoning involved, will always win out if given the opportunity to air itself. The Chinese government does not intend to offer that luxury to its people.

And herein lies a basic dilemma perennially looming on the Chinese horizon—and one that the United States must be very well aware of.

China has so indoctrinated its youthful charges as to its position on Taiwan, and the kids have been so thoroughly brainwashed into thinking that this is of the utmost national importance, even more so when international *Face* is taken into account, that they would gladly volunteer to defend Mainland China's right to claim Taiwan under the communist boot heel *en masse*. They wouldn't even question it.

The Chinese Communist Propaganda Machine has done a very commendable job of propagandizing their "right" to invade Taiwan and by making the topic taboo, and in all instances "non-debatable," they have secured a very valuable ace up their sleeve as a powerful future international bargaining tool.

If all else fails within the Chinese mainland the government can always stir up trouble in Taiwan and direct all national focus toward the conquest of that country, in the name of national unity and the preservation of international *Face*.

Let there be no mistake regarding this point. China, and its hundreds of millions of misguided citizens, would blindly go to battle for Taiwan if the government deemed it necessary. And with one fourth of the population—over 300,000,000 (the entire population of the United States)—15 years of age or younger, the concept of an eventual physical invasion becomes abundantly clear.

The United States, and its allies, must never sell this idea short.

And with all due respect to allied fighting forces throughout the world—to send them to fight on Chinese soil—be it the mainland or Taiwan—all invading armies would be totally annihilated.

The Chinese government knows this full well—and would not hesitate to unleash the Chinese populace in a maniacal charge to "rescue" Taiwan *from* democracy—if it meant the survival of the Chinese Communist Party.

Please recall, the CCP is the main focus of its national flag— not the people.

China is Dead Serious About Taiwan

In an article by David Lague of the *International Herald Tribune*, published August 8, 2006 on the Internet, "China executed a top official accused of spying for Taiwan and then distributed videotapes of his trial around the country as a warning to other civil servants, according to reports on government websites.

"The official, Tong Daning, was a department head at China's $26 billion national pension fund, the National Council for Social Security Fund. The reports said Mr. Tong was executed in April.

"He was the most senior Chinese official to be executed for espionage since Lt. Gen. Liu Liangkun in 1999; he, too, was accused of supplying secrets to Taiwan.

"Mainland China and Taiwan have a long history of spying on one another, especially concerning military preparations on either side of the Taiwan Strait.

"The Communist regime in Beijing regards Taiwan as a renegade Chinese province, not a separate country, while the democratic regime in Taiwan still regards itself, formally at least, as the legitimate government of all China.

"Taiwan has not declared independence, and Beijing has refused to rule out the use of force to reunite the two if such a declaration is made.

"The provincial office of China's State Secrets Bureau organized the screening, the report said. It gave no specific details of the accusations against Mr. Tong, but said that the video revealed 'startling facts' that served as a warning to others.

"The State Secrets Bureau operates at all levels of the country's sprawling civil service to guard confidential information. Experts on the Chinese bureaucracy say the bureau plays an important role in a government that routinely demands that even the most mundane information remain confidential."

Mr Lague continues in this very compelling report by saying, "At the same time, China is building up its armed forces facing Taiwan across the strait, a development that most experts believe is rapidly tilting the balance of power in the mainland's favor. In this environment of threat and opportunity, both sides have a strong need to step up their intelligence gathering, analysts say.

"For Beijing, the growing Taiwanese presence on the mainland presents a challenge to Chinese security services responsible for detecting spies. There are regular reports in the state-controlled press about the exposure of accused spies for Taiwan."

To buttress Mr. Lague's argument, according to the *2006 China Military Power Report*, "China has retained its long-standing focus on rival Taiwan but years of double-digit growth in arms spending and new missiles, ships and aircraft meant it could project power further afield."

The report goes on to point out that, "The pace and scope of China's military build-up already place regional military balances at risk.

"Current trends in China's military modernization could provide China with a force capable of prosecuting a range of military operations in Asia—well beyond Taiwan—potentially posing a credible threat to modern militaries operating in the region.

"China, which has claimed Taiwan as its own since 1949, has vowed to attack the self-ruled democratic island if it formally declares independence. The United States is obliged by law to help Taiwan defend itself."

To further demonstrate how serious China is about the Taiwan issue, an Internet article from BEIJING (AFP) Thursday, March 8, 2007, confirmed that, "China's defence budget will soar by a massive 17.8 percent in 2007, a senior official announced Sunday, as the United States said it wanted to know more about the Asian giant's intentions.

"China's armed forces will get 350.9 billion Yuan (about 45 billion dollars) for 2007, a rise of nearly 53 billion Yuan over actual spending in 2006," said Jiang Enzhu, a spokesman for the National People's Congress.

Jiang went on to explain that, "The military expenditure would account for 7.5 percent of total government expenditure in 2007, compared with 7.4 percent in 2006."

He also reiterated that, "Constitutional reform efforts by Taiwan President Chen Shui-bian were moving the democratic island dangerously towards formal independence, and warned against such moves.

"To resolutely contain the separatist activities of Taiwan independence forces and safeguard peace in the Taiwan Strait is the most important and urgent task facing compatriots on both sides of the strait," Jiang said.

"China will never tolerate an independent Taiwan and will never permit anyone under any form to split Taiwan from the mainland."

There should be no further question as to how serious the Chinese Communist Party is on the point of Taiwan.

With this in mind another question arises. Since Taiwan was annexed in 1683 (but has never been physically connected to the mainland) and Tibet came under China's control in the mid 1700s, then what is to stop China from exercising its "historical right" to reclaim Burma, Nepal, Korea and "Outer Mongolia?"

Beyond that precarious scenario, are we then to consider China's ancient dispute/claim that the island of Okinawa (Japan) is also part of their sovereign territory?

For America, the line of democracy will not be drawn in the sands of the Middle East, but in China—in the sand on the beaches of Taiwan. If America does not uphold its end of the bargain to protect Taiwan if attacked by Mainland China—every national security contract the USA has with every other country will simply become "null and void" and a new world order—or disorder—will ultimately emerge.

It would be a disaster of epic proportions if the United States of America would allow Taiwan to become the Sacrificial Lamb on the alter of International Globalism.

SOURCES:

"Coming Over the Horizon—Why China Wants a Bigger Navy," *The Economist*, January 6, 2007, pg.34

"Shot Across Our Bow, Defense: China's President Announces that the World's Most Populous Nation is Preparing to Challenge U.S. Naval Supremacy on the High Seas by Building a Blue-Water Navy, the Dragon Sets Sail," *Investor's Business Daily*, ISSUES & INSIGHTS, Wednesday, January 3, 2007, pg. A12

CHAPTER 10

THE GREAT LEAP BACKWARD

The following information was directly retrieved via the Internet, from the Amnesty International website. The reports and information that follow are edited due to the size and scope of the information contained therein. However, it is hoped that the reader will get some idea of the calculated magnitude of governmental suppression that is now underway in the "New" China of today.

For the full context of the articles herein please refer to the Amnesty International website at http://www.amnesty.org

People's Republic of China Controls Tighten as Internet Activism Grows

"Internet access has expanded considerably in China over the past year. According to official statistics, the number of Internet users had risen to 79.5 million by December 2003 from 59.1 million users in December 2002—an increase of 34.5 percent. This has presented the authorities with greater challenges in their attempts to censor and control the online activities of Internet users. Over the past year, there has been a growing trend towards assigning greater responsibilities of surveillance and monitoring to a variety of companies in China such as Internet Cafes, Information Service Providers (ISPs) and other enterprises.

"Nevertheless, it appears that Internet activism is continuing to grow in China as fast as the controls are tightened. Over the last year, there have been signs of Internet users acting increasingly in solidarity with one another, in particular by expressing support for each other online. Such expressions of solidarity have proved dangerous, as a growing number of people have been detained on the basis of such postings.

"Signing online petitions, calling for reform and an end to corruption, planning to set up a pro-democracy party, publishing 'rumors about SARS,' communicating with groups abroad, opposing the persecution of the Falun Gong and calling for a review of the 1989 crackdown on the democracy protests are all examples of activities considered by the authorities to be 'subversive' or to 'endanger state security.' Such charges almost always result in prison sentences.

"Many of those included in this report have been held for long periods, sometimes for over a year, awaiting a formal trial and for some there has been a long delay between trial and sentencing. All are believed to have been denied full and adequate access to lawyers and their families, particularly during the initial stages of police detention, and several have reported being tortured or ill-treated. Such violations of the right to a fair trial and to freedom from torture or ill-treatment often contravene provisions of China's Criminal Procedure Law as well as international human rights standards.

"The following cases illustrate such failings. They also show how the arrest of one Internet activist can result in spiralling arrests of others who dare to express their support or solidarity online. Several of these cases have been documented by Amnesty International elsewhere. The information below is intended to bring their cases up to date and to show the systematic nature of state persecution of Internet activists."

1. Huang Qi, is notable for being the first person in China to be arrested for posting articles concerning human rights and political issues on his own website. After his trial in August 2001 he continued to be detained for almost two years before his sentence was finally announced on 9 May 2003 with five years imprisonment for "inciting subversion."

2. Liu Di, a psychology student from Beijing Normal University, was freed on bail on 28 November 2003 more than one year after her detention on 7 November 2002. Just before her release, it was announced that the public prosecutors in Beijing had rejected the case against her due to lack of evidence. Liu Di had been held incommunicado for over four months until she was allowed to meet her lawyer in March 2003, and her family was denied access to her throughout her detention. She was reportedly warned that the conditions for her release on bail were that she should not speak to foreign journalists or travel away from Beijing. On 25 December 2003 it was finally announced that she would not face formal indictment.

Unlike many of those detained for their online activities, Liu Di was not already known to be a political dissident—she was merely a student expressing her views online.

3. Cai Lujun, a businessman from Hebei Province and Luo Changfu, a laid-off worker from Chongqing Municipality, were both charged with subversion and sentenced to three years imprisonment in October 2003 and November 2003 respectively.

4. Du Daobin, a civil servant from Hubei Province and a prominent organizer of petitions in support of Liu Di, was also detained. He told journalists in October that "Detaining Liu Di is a violation of freedom of expression. Why do we still have literary persecution in the 21st century?" On 12 November 2003 Du Daobin was charged with "inciting subversion," but he has yet to face trial. Thousands in China and abroad have since signed two open letters to Chinese Premier Wen Jiabao calling for Du Daobin's release.

5. Kong Youping, a factory worker from Liaoning Province was detained on 13 December 2003 after he too had appealed for the release of Liu Di. He had also posted articles and poems on a foreign website and called for a reassessment of the 1989 pro-democracy demonstrations as well as an end to official corruption. To Amnesty International's knowledge he has yet to be charged.

6. Ouyang Yi, has had his case returned to prosecutors several times by the Chengdu Intermediate People's Court in Sichuan Province due to insufficient evidence. He was detained in December 2002 and charged with "incitement to subvert state power" after he had created a pro-democracy website and signed a petition, together with 192 other dissidents, addressed to the 16th Communist Party Congress calling for greater democracy and the release of dissidents arrested for publishing their views on the Internet.

Increased Controls and Surveillance of Internet Users

"China is said to have in place the most extensive censorship of the Internet of any country in the world.

"Many of the toughest regulations to control the Internet have been issued since 2000 and those who cause 'especially serious harm' by providing 'state secrets' to overseas organizations and individuals over the Internet can be sentenced to death.

"As all communication on the Internet in China passes through government-controlled routers, the authorities are able to block access to many sites and to filter content and delete individual links or web pages if considered 'dangerous' or 'subversive.'"

Corporate Responsibility and Internet Freedoms

Appeal Cases

"Within their respective spheres of activity and influence, transnational corporations and other business enterprises have the obligation to promote, secure the fulfilment, ensure respect of and protect human rights recognized in international as well as national law, including the rights and interests of indigenous peoples and other vulnerable groups.

"As China's burgeoning economy grows and with its admission in December 2001 to the World Trade Organization (WTO), foreign ownership, investment and involvement of foreign companies in

China's telecommunications industry have soared.

"Amnesty International remains concerned that in their pursuit of new and lucrative markets, foreign corporations may be indirectly contributing to human rights violations or at the very least failing to give adequate consideration to the human rights implications of their investments. In its first report on *State Control of the Internet in China*, Amnesty International cited several foreign companies (Cisco Systems, Microsoft, Nortel Networks, Websense and Sun Microsystems), which had reportedly provided technology which has been used to censor and control the use of the Internet in China."

SOURCE:

United Nations Human Rights Norms for Businesses, Adopted 13 August 2003, Geneva

The People List

The following is just a smattering of people who have been detained—or murdered—while in the hands of governmental authorities. It should be noted that this list is, in no way whatsoever, complete. These are just a few who represent the democracy movement in the "New" China of today.

Unofficial estimates of Chinese citizens being illegally incarcerated run into the *hundreds of thousands*.

As with everything else in China it is virtually impossible to ensure that "official numbers" are statistically correct, let alone independently verifiable.

However, this partial listing of the names of detainees has been, for the most part, verified and is considered to be factually accurate by Amnesty International. Due to space limitations, it is impossible to list every single detainee. It is hoped that the reader will get a sense of what is going on by this admittedly very small listing of incarcerated— or exterminated—Chinese citizens.

Again, for the most part, this information is taken directly from the Amnesty International website.

1. He Depu, aged 47, was detained on 4 November 2002 for posting essays on the Internet and for his links with the banned China Democracy Party (CDP). He was sentenced to eight years imprisonment on 6 November 2003.

He Depu's health has reportedly deteriorated while in prison, he has lost a lot of weight and is suffering from hepatitis for which he has reportedly received no treatment.

He Depu, an academic, was once employed at the prestigious research institute, the Chinese Academy of Social Sciences. He has long been involved in dissident activities going back to the Democracy Wall protests in 1979.

2. Huang Qi, a computer engineer from Sichuan, who set up his own website, was detained on 3 June 2000 after several Chinese dissidents abroad posted articles on his website on the eve of the 11th anniversary of the crackdown against the 1989 pro-democracy protests. Three years after his arrest he was sentenced to five years of imprisonment after an unfair trial.

He has been badly beaten by prison guards and is now in poor health suffering from regular headaches.

Huang Qi set up his website in 1998 to help family members trace missing relatives. The website also included reports about the independence movement in the Xinjiang Uighur Autonomous Region and the Falun Gong spiritual movement. Huang Qi is considered to be the first known webmaster in China to be arrested and tried for publishing human rights and political material on his own website.

3. Jin Haike, Xu Wei, Yang Zili and Zhang Honghai were sentenced on 28 May 2003 each to prison terms of between eight and ten years after posting articles of political and social concern on the Internet.

The four were detained on 13 March 2001 and charged with "subverting state power and the overthrow of the socialist system" after they set up the New Youth Study Group (*Xin Qingnian Xuehu*), an organization which advocated social and democratic reform, including the promotion and observance of democratic voting procedures in the election of village committees.

According to the indictment, the group was illegal, had met secretly and had proposed that "the current political regime in China had to be altered, change of society had to be achieved and a liberal social system had to be re-established."

Their trial was held at the Beijing Intermediate People's Court on 28 September 2001 but adjourned after four hours for further investigation. It was reconvened at the Beijing Intermediate People's Court in April 2003. During the trial Xu Wei complained about abusive treatment in prison, including being beaten and tortured with electric shocks to his genitals, causing long-term numbness to his lower body. To Amnesty International's knowledge, no official investigation has been carried out into these allegations.

4. Yang Zili, a writer and computer engineer, also had his own website, "Yang Zili's Garden of Ideas," where he posted poems, essays and reports. The website was shut down by the authorities shortly after his arrest.

5. Luo Yongzhong, a 36-year-old disabled shopkeeper, was detained for publishing articles and opinions on the Internet. He was later charged with "endangering state security" and tried by the Changchun Intermediate People's Court in mid-October 2003. He was sentenced to three years in prison.

At the time of Luo Yongzhong's arrest on 13 June 2003 the police searched his house and confiscated his computer, printer and some of the articles he had posted on the Internet. These articles advocated constitutional reform to protect human rights and free speech, and criticized the "Three Represents" and the way the government dealt with the Severe Acute Respiratory Syndrome (SARS) outbreak.

One of Luo's articles was entitled *Tell Today's Youth the Truth about June 4*—a reference to the crackdown on the pro-democracy demonstrations in Tiananmen Square in 1989. This article was one of several which were used as evidence to convict Luo Yongzhong.

Luo's articles were also published on the Chinese language website Boxun News (*Boxun Xinwen*), based in the United States. Luo, who is lame in one leg, had also written a number of articles advocating better rights for disabled people.

According to the judgment, Luo had written several essays between May and June 2003 which "attacked the socialist system, incited the subversion of state power and created a negative influence on society."

6. Tao Haidong, a 45-year-old writer was sentenced in January 2003 to seven years of imprisonment after publishing articles critical of the government on the Internet.

Tao Haidong was charged with "incitement to subvert state power" after being held incommunicado for several months following his arrest on 9 July 2002. He was tried in secret on 8 January 2003 by the Urumqi Intermediate People's Court in the Xinjiang Uighur Autonomous Region (XUAR), northwest China.

The court reportedly found that Tao Haidong had written three books, which "brazenly defamed and insulted Party and State leaders." These books predicted China's economy was near collapse and described China as the world's largest base of feudalism. Extracts from these books were said to have been posted on websites based in China and abroad.

7. Cai Lujun, subversion, 3 year sentence, businessman, signed an online petition demanding the release of Liu Di. He also wrote essays on problems affecting farmers and calling for democratic reforms.

8. Chen Shaowen, subversion, sentence not known, writer and former police officer, posted up to 40 "reactionary" articles on the Internet.

9. Chi Shouzhu, sentence not known, student, printed pro-democracy material from the Internet.

10. Dong Yanhong, 5 year sentence, downloading material from Falun Gong websites and disseminating information on Falun Gong. Secret trial, Falun Gong practitioner.

11. Du Daobin, sentence not known, signed an online petition asking for the release of Liu Di and organized a "mock detention" campaign for her support. Also posted several articles on the Internet on social and political issues. Thousands have signed an open letter calling for his release.

12. Guo Qinghai, 4 year sentence, journalist, published essays on the Internet regarding Qi Yanchen's case. Qi, convicted for "subversion and diffusion of anti-governmental news via the Internet," was released early in May 2003.

13. Huang Kui, sentence not known, student, posted articles opposing the persecution of Falun Gong on the Internet. Falun Gong practitioner.

14. Huang Qunwei, 3 years, unemployed, posted essays on SARS on the Internet.

15. Jiang Lijun, 4 year sentence, occupation not known, advocated democracy on the Internet and intended to organize a political party. Suspected of being a ringleader of online pro-democracy activism.

16. Jiang Yuxia, verdict has not been announced, student, posted articles opposing the persecution of Falun Gong on the Internet. Falun Gong practitioner.

17. Kong Youping, sentence not known, factory employee, posted articles and poems on an overseas website calling for an end to corruption and reassessment of the 1989 pro-democracy movement, and called for the release of Liu Di. Member of the China Democracy Party.

18. Li Chunyan, verdict has not been announced, student, posted articles opposing the persecution of Falun Gong on the Internet. Falun Gong practitioner.

19. Li Dawei, 11 year sentence, former police officer, downloaded materials from Chinese Democracy websites overseas, and compiled them into a book.

20. Li Hongmin, sentence not known, occupation not known, posted articles on the Internet on the crackdown on the 1989 pro-democracy movement.

21. Li Yanfang, verdict has not been announced, student, posted articles opposing the persecution of Falun Gong on the Internet. Falun Gong practitioner.

22. Li Zhi, 8 year sentence, civil servant, communicated with overseas dissidents via chat rooms, accused officials of corruption.

23. Lin Yang, verdict has not been announced, student, posted articles opposing the persecution of Falun Gong on the Internet. Falun Gong practitioner.

24. Liu Haofeng, 3 year sentence to re-education through labour, journalist, wrote two articles that appeared on China Democracy Party website based in California. Member of the China Democracy Party.

25. Liu Weifang, 3 year sentence, shopkeeper and essayist, posted essays critical of the government on the Internet under a pseudonym "LGWF."

26. Liu Wenyu, 3 year sentence, graduate student, downloading material from Falun Gong websites and disseminating information on Falun Gong. Secret trial. Falun Gong practitioner.

27. Lu Xinhua, 4 year sentence, occupation not known, posted articles on the Internet about corrupt village officials. Member of the

China Democracy Party.

28. Luo Changfu, 3 year sentence, laid-off worker, posted articles on the Internet calling for the release of Liu Di under a pseudonym "Justice and Consciousness."

29. Ma Yan, verdict has not been announced, student, posted articles opposing the persecution of Falun Gong on the Internet. Falun Gong practitioner.

30. Mao Qingxiang, 8 year sentence, occupation not known, published a magazine called *Opposition Party* and distributed pro-democracy writings online to groups overseas. Was transferred to a hospital in December 2002 after his health deteriorated in prison. Member of the China Democracy Party.

31. Meng Jun, 10 year sentence, lecturer, downloading material from Falun Gong websites and disseminating information on Falun Gong. Secret trial. Falun Gong practitioner. Reportedly ill-treated and tortured.

32. Mu Chuanheng, 3 year sentence, writer and lawyer, main contributor to the online forum *New Culture Forum*. Called for the release of Yan Peng who was detained in July 2001 and later sentenced to 18 months of imprisonment and 2 years deprivation of political rights. Yan Peng is now presumed released. He was one of the first Chinese dissidents to use the Internet to express his views, and taught others to use it.

33. Ouyang Yi, sentence not known, former teacher, created a pro-democracy website and signed a petition addressed to the 16th Communist Party Congress that was later posted on the Internet, calling for democracy. Member of the China Democracy Party. The sentencing of Ouyang Yi has been postponed due to lack of evidence.

34. Quan Huicheng, 3 year sentence, occupation unknown, downloaded, photocopied and distributed material from overseas Falun Gong websites. Falun Gong practitioner.

35. Sang Jiancheng, 3 year sentence, retired worker, posted an article on the Internet accusing the Chinese government of corruption and signed a petition addressed to the 16th Communist Party Congress that was later posted on the Internet, calling for democracy.

36. Tan Qiu, sentence not known, former hospital worker, distributed "reactionary" messages on the Internet.

37. Wang Jinbo, 4 year sentence, former employee of a pharmaceutical company, E-mailed articles to overseas organizations calling for a re-evaluation of the 1989 Tiananmen protests and the release of political prisoners in China. Member of the China Democracy Party. Tortured and ill-treated.

38. Wang Sen, 10 year sentence, occupation not known, detained after posting on the Internet an allegation that a local medical center sold Red Cross donated medicine at inflated prices. Formally convicted and sentenced for organizing workers protest in December 2000. Member of the China Democracy Party.

39. Wang Xin, 9 year sentence, student, downloading material from Falun Gong websites and disseminating information on Falun Gong. Secret trial. Falun Gong practitioner.

40. Wang Xuefei, 11 year sentence, student, downloading material from Falun Gong websites and disseminating information on Falun Gong. Secret trial. Falun Gong practitioner.

41. Wang Zhenyong, sentence unknown, university professor, distributed material on Falun Gong on the Internet. Falun Gong practitioner.

42. Wu Yilong, 11 year sentence, occupation not known, published a magazine called *Opposition Party* and distributed pro-democracy materials online to groups overseas. Member of the China Democracy Party.

43. Xu Wei, 10 year sentence, reporter and editor, posted articles of

political and social concerns on the Internet. Tortured and ill-treated.

44. Xu Guang, 5 year sentence, occupation not known, published a magazine called *Opposition Party* and distributed pro-democracy materials online to groups overseas. Member of the China Democracy Party.

45. Yan Jun, 2 year sentence, biology teacher, posted material critical of the government and especially the crackdown of the 1989 pro-democracy movement, and advocated greater democracy on the Internet. Went missing in April 2003. Secret trial. Beaten repeatedly by fellow detainees, reportedly acting on orders from the police in July 2003.

46. Yao Yue, 12 year sentence, graduate student, downloaded material from Falun Gong websites and disseminated information on Falun Gong. Secret trial. Falun Gong practitioner.

47. Zhang Haitao, sentence not known, computer engineer, created a China-based Falun Gong website. Falun Gong practitioner.

48. Zhang Honghai, 8 year sentence, freelance writer, posted articles of political and social concerns on the Internet.

49. Zhang Ji, sentence not known, student, distributed material on the situation of the Falun Gong in Heilongjiang Province to overseas website. Falun Gong practitioner.

50. Zhang Shengqi, sentence not known, computer firm employee, posted articles supporting a banned Christian church on the Internet.

51. Zhang Yuhui, 10 year sentence, businessman, posted articles on Falun Gong to both domestic and overseas websites. Secret trial. Falun Gong practitioner. Reportedly tortured and ill-treated.

52. Zhang Yuxiang, sentence not known, former armed forces official, detained for interrogation about the articles he posted on the Internet.

53. Zheng, sentence not known, occupation not known, used a pseudonym "Sini." Believed to have posted "harmful information" on the Internet.

54. Zhu Yufu, 7 year sentence, occupation not known, posted "harmful information" on an Internet chatroom. Published a magazine called *Opposition Party* and distributed pro-democracy materials online to groups overseas. Member of the China Democracy Party.

And Those Who Didn't Make It

55. Chen Qiulan, sentence not known, occupation not known, posted material on Falun Gong on the Internet. Falun Gong practitioner. Died in custody on 24 August 2001.

56. Li Changjun, sentence not known, civil servant, downloaded material on Falun Gong from the Internet. Falun Gong practitioner. Reportedly tortured in custody. His family was informed on 27 June 2001 that he was dead.

57. Xue Hairong, 7 year sentence, occupation not known, downloaded material on Falun Gong from the Internet. Falun Gong practitioner. Reportedly died of leukemia when in custody on 22 March 2001. Amnesty International has not been able to independently confirm the information about his death or access to medical treatment.

58. Zhao Chunying, sentence not known, occupation not known, arrested and reportedly beaten to death by police after she posted on the Internet an account of being tortured during a previous detention. Her family was informed on 10 May 2003 that she was dead. Falun Gong practitioner.

SOURCE:

Amnesty International: International Secretariat, 1 Easton Street, London WC1X0DW, United Kingdom. All information was either directly or indirectly sourced from the Internet and credit for this compilation of information is therefore due Amnesty International. Any mistakes in spelling or other inaccuracies are those of the author.

NOTE: As mentioned earlier, this list is far from complete. Information and the whereabouts of scores of other Chinese citizens remains a mystery. There are numerous estimates—all very difficult to confirm—regarding Chinese citizens that have been abducted by the police or the military, disappeared under mysterious circumstances at the hands of local party officials or simply murdered and disposed of in unmarked graves in the surrounding countryside.

Terrorists or Dissidents?

In an article by Jason Dean, he states that, "China's government said police killed 18 terrorists and destroyed a training camp connected with Islamic separatists, marking an apparent escalation of Beijing's struggle against antigovernment elements in the country's restive northwest."

The article went on to point out that, "Some foreign experts and human-rights advocates say China's government exaggerates the terrorist connections of anti-government elements in the region as a cover to crack down on all dissent—a charge Chinese officials have denied."

SOURCE:

Dean, Jason "China Says Police Kill 18 Terrorists," *The Wall Street Journal*, Tuesday, January 9, 2007, pg. A4

Madame Tussaud's Macabre Chinese House of Horrors

I must admit that I was stunned when I came across the following article in the *Epoch Times* entitled, "Genocide and Olympics cannot coexist in China," written by Sarah Matheson.

The author states that there is very convincing evidence that, "A state-sanctioned genocide campaign is seizing organs from Falun Gong practitioners and selling them for high prices."

It is no secret that Falun Gong members are persecuted in China. To be a member is against the law and can lead to a death sentence.

But what is shocking are that more and more authoritative reports of "short waiting times that have been advertised for perfectly-matched organs would suggest the existence of a computerized matching system for transplants and a large bank of live, prospective donors."

UN special reporter Manfred Nowak, in his summary on human rights abuses in China, concludes his chilling report by stating that, "It is alleged that the discrepancy between available organs and numbers from unidentifiable sources is explained by organs harvested from Falun Gong practitioners, and that the rise in transplants from 2000 coincides and correlates with the beginning of the persecution of these persons."

If this report is even partially true it *should* signal to the rest of the world that not only is the current Communist Chinese Dynasty abhorrently tyrannical in its treatment of its own citizens but that they are no less barbaric and sinister than their Japanese captors during their occupation of China from the mid 1930s to the end of World War Two.

I would encourage every reader to follow up on these reports to see if they can be justified and further documented. If this turns out to be factual it is imperative that the United States—as well as the rest of the "civilized world"—immediately move to expel the People's Republic of China from the United Nations, the World Trade Organization, the IMF, and be publicly stripped of their seat on the United Nations Human Rights Commission.

To do anything less would be tantamount to aiding and abetting an outlaw renegade nation.

SOURCE:

Matheson, Sarah "Genocide and Olympics cannot co-exist in China," *The Epoch Times*, May 15–28, 2007, pg.1

THE COMING REVOLUTION

An article by Thomas Lum states that, "A wave of social unrest is sweeping across China—in the past two years, the number of public protests has risen by nearly 50%—and the government has been 'unable or unwilling' to control the eruptions, according to a new report prepared by the Congressional Research Service."

The report goes on to say, "Peasants and farmers are unhappy with the environmental degradation, official corruption, and decline in employment and social services that followed the decollectivization of state agriculture, and they are resisting the government's attempts to seize property and force evictions for infrastructure projects."

SOURCE:

"Primary Sources," *The Atlantic Monthly*, October 2006, pg. 42 as reported in, "Social Unrest in China," by Thomas Lum, Congressional Research Service.

PRE-EPILOG

It would not be fair, nor would it be journalistically appropriate, to point out all the bad points in China without offering a few suggestions of my own.

The only thing wrong with this assumption is its innate Western arrogance in assuming that I could offer anything that might help China. I can't.

China will have to help herself—and that is the main problem with the "New" China of today.

The Chinese Communist Party has been in control for over 60 years—and it does not intend to give up one ounce of its power base without a fight.

During the reign of the present Chinese Communist Dynasty, it has been engaged in round after round of corruption, gone from one financial catastrophe to another, overseen mass famine and flooding that has killed tens of millions, had the supreme audacity to murder its own students calling for democracy in 1989—and yet, it still tenaciously clings to power by any means available.

The Chinese Communist Party doesn't need me to tell it that they should reinstate national healthcare—for free—for the sake of the People.

The Chinese Communist Party already knows this.

The Chinese Communist Party doesn't need me to tell it that they should reinstate education for every child—for free—for the sake of the People.

The Chinese Communist Party already knows this.

And the Chinese Communist Party doesn't need me to tell them to stop stealing the People's land.

The fact of the matter is, the Chinese Communist Party does not care about the People.

If it did, it never would have reneged on its promise of all-encompassing socialism in the first place.

The ones at the top are taking as much as they can with the full knowledge that the Chinese Communist Party is well on its way to total demise.

Only time will tell how much the People really care about China and what they will choose to do about rescuing their own country from the despotic grip of the present Chinese Communist Dynasty.

It is up to the People—and the People alone.

EPILOG

"Those who make peaceful revolution impossible will make violent revolution inevitable."

JOHN F. KENNEDY

Rapid change in China comes very slowly. When people are divided the status quo is safe. When people are united they are dangerous.

At present, Chinese people no longer work for a living—they work to survive.

Thanks to worldwide systemic corruption, international benign neglect and the pious duplicity of Globalization, China has been successfully turned into the sweatshop of the world.

With 1,000,000,000 people constantly on the brink of starvation, the world mega-corporations have a slave labor force that can produce cheap goods for pennies on the dollar, sell the finished products at bargain-basement prices, bank the exorbitant profits while sharing nothing with the invisible Chinese people who are forced to either work just to survive, or go without—and perish.

China is a classic example of a house of cards—a gigantic Ponzi scheme being perpetrated on an international scale—which keeps feeding upon itself in exponential fashion. Sooner, rather than later, there will be nothing left to eat, and China will devour itself into utter chaos and confusion—like so many times before.

In this concerted, frighteningly methodical approach to acquire unconscionable profits from the backs of the faceless, hundreds of millions of people, the international economic gang rape, under the guise of benevolent Globalization, is now in full swing.

My disappointment is not with the Chinese people. It is with the Globalization of systematic, meticulous manipulation that they are forced to endure under.

I am sorely disappointed with the mass media and its obscuring of the facts through intentional *news abuse* in their, mostly glowing, reports of what is really taking place in China.

And I must admit that, as a teacher, I am disappointed in myself for having first been a huge supporter of the concept of Globalization. It wasn't until I finally saw the horrible way in which the "average" Chinese is forced to exist that I actually started to question how China could make products at such a discount to the rest of the world.

I thought I had Globalization all figured out. But only after living in China, and seeing what it actually entails, did it even begin to dawn on me that Globalization is the perfect way to eradicate competition on an international level, through the explicit use of forced, slave labor, by mega-rich corporations in conjunction with private equity acquisition firms, under the ever-repressive, watchful eye of the Chinese Communist Party.

As we sit and debate inane topics of little social significance, these global bandits are gobbling up all competitive entities still available. Once the competition is decimated, prices will rise to such heights that we will some day look back upon oil at $90 a barrel and reminisce about the "good old days."

Why is there no International Sherman Anti-trust Act?

Because the WTO, IMF, UN and the World Bank are in on the worldwide scam. They are leading all "average" people down the road to international economic servitude.

For once competition is gone—we will all be slaves to the Corporate Establishment of International Globalization. It is already starting to happen.

Do the American people really think only of money and nothing else, as they are so often accused?

Has the concept of American fairness and the rule of law descended to such a level that our leaders no longer care?

There has not been one voice in the United States Congress that has *consistently* spoken up for the 1,000,000,000 Chinese people held in literal bondage by the Chinese Communist Party.

Is it possible that the disdain in which America is held today, in so many parts of the world, is actually justified?

America—a nation of cowards—afraid to condemn China for unimaginable human rights abuses that are continuing to this very day.

America can be outspoken, belligerent, aggressive and pugnacious concerning ever-mounting human rights violations when it comes to tiny Cuba, and more recently Vietnam.

However, when it comes to China—and the billions of United States dollar denominated debt that the Chinese Communist Party has agreed to fund—provided that the USA doesn't complain—only adds to the perception of America as a heartless, international bully.

Martin Luther Jr. once said that, "Injustice anywhere is a threat to justice everywhere."

America, as the only superpower on earth and the leader of the Free World, owes it to the enslaved Chinese to take a leading roll in speaking out in behalf of, *We the People*.

For if this obvious abuse of human rights is allowed to continue unabated in China—in the name of Globalization—what is to keep it from contaminating the rest of the free world?

Every chance American leaders get, they should rile at the mistreatment that the Chinese people are forced to exist under—not only on the floors of the United States Senate and the House of Representatives— but also at the podium in the United Nations General Assembly.

If *Face* is really as important as I think it is, public condemnation, continuous humiliation in the international arena, would work wonders.

After all, the Chinese Communist Party wants nothing more than to be loved and admired by the rest of the world. They are thirsting for it.

Where is the compassion that America once stood so proudly for?

Where is the outrage of the average American citizen?

Only time will tell if the hidden shame of the People's Republic of China will ever be revealed.

It is my sincere hope that CHINA HOUSE will, in some small way, help to shed light on what is really happening to the great working masses of the "New" China.

May God bless China, and her People, in the hopes that truth will someday prevail.

ISBN 141207066-X